Staudt
on
Sports

Tim Staudt

Published by
Visions Sports & Publishing, Inc.
1998

© 1998 Visions Sports & Publishing, Inc.

Visions Sports & Publishing, Inc.
P.O. Box 338, East Lansing, Michigan 48826-0338
(517) 485-0848

Cover and interior design by: Camron Gnass
Edited by: Lisa Gagarin

Printed by Walsworth in the United States of America
First Printing: August 1998

ISBN: 0-9658933-9-1

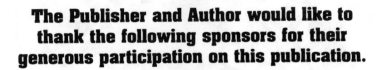

The Publisher and Author would like to thank the following sponsors for their generous participation on this publication.

Farm Bureau
Hot-N-Now
Royal Scot
Sneekers Restaurant
Liskey's
Hawk Hallow
Poppa Leo's Pizza
Emil's Italian Restaurant
WVFN Radio 730AM The Fan
Jackson National Life
Gadaleto Ramsby & Associates
Dean Charters & Tours
Williams Auto World
MSU Bookstore
WILX TV NBC-10
Carpet Man
621 E. Michigan Avenue

The Grand Hotel
on Mackinaw Island
Drolett Travel
Golf Haus
Falcon Productions

Vision Creative
The Sports Outlet
Norman Gaffney
Contemporary Audio

POPPA LEO'S PIZZA

Family owned & operated
Established 1986

Lansing's

Hometown Pizza

7 area stores to serve you!

SNEEKERS
RESTAURANT

The "Hometown Ribs" That Are Simply
The Best Again And Again...

517 337-9201

emíl's

ITALIAN RESTAURANT

●

_____

SERVING YOU
FOR OVER
75 YEARS

_____

●

(517) 482-4430

DEDICATION

I would like to salute two charities which are near and dear to my heart, and have been throughout my career. When I agreed to write this book for the publisher, I decided that all of the remuneration I would receive would be split between the Children's Miracle Network and the Greater Lansing Food Bank. Both of them serve thousands of people in the area who are in need of help.

The Children's Miracle Network (CMN) was created in 1989, with WILX-TV as a host from the beginning. I have witnessed numerous children who have been nursed back to health thanks to CMN. Lansing's Sparrow Hospital is an affiliated member of CMN. In the last nine years, the annual CMN telethon has raised several million dollars toward the hospital's pediatric services. Dr. Stephen Guertin, who heads up Sparrow's Pediatric Unit, is one of the finest human beings that I have ever met. I have told him that if something ever happens to my children and they need immediate treatment, he has my blessing and approval to do what he needs to in order to help them.

Sparrow Hospital treats children free of charge if their families do not have the economic means to pay for their care. The hospital has never been given its public due for all it has done for the children it has helped. God bless CMN and Sparrow Hospital.

The Greater Lansing Food Bank has been guided over the years by Camille Abood, a kind, dedicated and caring man who has served the community for many years. He has resolved to help people in economic distress via the food bank and has helped raise millions of dollars over the years. He has attracted many talented and dedicated volunteers to the cause and has won me over with his commitment.

This book is dedicated to these two worthy charities and the wonderful individuals who support them. The proceeds from this book may only help them in a minor way, but both will always be major players in the betterment of our community.

ACKNOWLEDGMENTS

I was surprised and pleased in late 1997 when the good people at Visions Sports & Publishing asked me for a meeting and to consider writing this book. I had been thinking about authoring a book for some time.

I met with Jon Harpst, who introduced me to Vision Sports President and CEO, Mike Ward. After several meetings, the project was off and running.

Editor Lisa Gagarin and I juggled our own hectic schedules to edit a manuscript that was easy to write, but much tougher for her to edit.

In writing this book, my family helped me learn enough about writing on a computer that I only lost a couple of chapters along the way.

Joe Falls of the Detroit News, a long-time friend, has given me advice over the years on a variety of issues. This project sent me to him for more.

Earvin Johnson readily agreed to help out with the foreword and his words are very much appreciated.

I can't begin to thank all the people who I've met over the years, because sure as heck I'd forget someone noteworthy. While I was alone at my computer, I would remember people and stories that had to be added later and made Lisa's job just that much tougher.

I want to thank all the community sponsors who Paul Nolan and Doug Cooper met with concerning this book.

These are my own words and feelings. I thank you, the reader, listener and viewer for all your support over the years.

Whether you like this book or not, at least you have helped two better causes: The Greater Lansing Food Bank and the Children's Miracle Network. Both have been very supportive throughout this entire project.

CONTENTS

ABOUT THE AUTHOR

Tim Staudt is one of the most experienced sportscasters in all of Michigan. He began his on-air career at the former WSWM radio in East Lansing while attending Michigan State University in 1969. While still in school he joined the news staff at WJIM radio. He soon added the duties of weather caster on the 11 p.m. television news at the old WJIM-TV, the CBS affiliate in Lansing, from November 1970 through April 1971. One month later, he was named sports director and has been on mid-Michigan television sets anchoring sportscasts ever since.

In July 1980, he joined the staff of WILX-TV with which he has a contract which takes him through April 2003.

No other broadcast personality, radio or television, has been on the air in mid-Michigan longer than Tim. In 1996, Detroit News columnist Joe Falls wrote that Staudt "is the best sportscaster in the state."

He has hosted his popular Staudt on Sports radio show since March 8, 1993, on WVFM AM 730. It airs weekdays at noon.

Staudt is a veteran play-by-play announcer dating back to Earvin Johnson's years at Lansing Everett High School in the mid-1970s through his college career as a Spartan. He has been a voice on the Big Ten television network in both basketball and football since 1990.

Staudt attended East Lansing High School and graduated from Michigan State University with a journalism degree in July 1971. He is married to Cathy, a kindergarten teacher, and they parent three boys, Thomas, Matthew and Patrick. His free time passion is golf, especially when played with his family.

FOREWORD

BY EARVIN "MAGIC" JOHNSON

It has been 23 years since I began my basketball career as a sophomore at Lansing Everett High School. I met Tim Staudt midway through that first varsity season as he broadcast many of our games on WJIM-AM radio. We became good friends over the years. When I was deciding on which college to attend, he kept pestering me along with all the other reporters about my future plans. I tease him to this day because he seemed to believe all along that Michigan was the college where I would play. I had fun keeping him guessing about it all.

Tim's first basketball television play-by-play experience began when I played my two seasons with the Spartans. He called a number of our games, and it was helpful to all those fans who could not get tickets to watch us perform in sold-out Jenison Fieldhouse. Our friendship continued to grow.

When Tim switched television stations back in 1980, I agreed to do some promos for him and we had fun at the taping session outside Everett High School. I had just completed my rookie season with the Los Angeles Lakers and was back home for a portion of that summer. Whenever I return home we try to visit at least once and we enjoy reminiscing over old times.

In 1986, I invited Tim, his wife Cathy and some of their friends to visit my Los Angeles home. We spent an afternoon together after they attended a Lakers' game. I introduced them to my teammates in the Lakers' locker room after we beat the Chicago Bulls in what was Michael Jordan's rookie season.

Even though I do not return to Lansing as often as I once did we still stay in touch whenever possible. I have always been impressed with the way Tim has covered so many different sports and teams over his 30 years in broadcasting. He has been around the sports scene throughout Michigan and the Big Ten for quite a while and few others in his business have witnessed so many different memorable events.

I was pleased that he asked me to write the foreword to this book. He has a rich background of great stories to tell from all of his experiences, which you should enjoy a great deal. Thirty years is a long time to do anything and many people have not heard him recall all the interesting stories he has witnessed.

In my promos seen on his television station, I have always referred to him as the "magic man of Michigan sports." He is truly that and he has meant a lot to the entire Mid-Michigan community. I have always enjoyed and appreciated Tim's honest professionalism and the great care and feelings he has for other people.

For all the people I have met around the world, Tim Staudt still holds a special place in my heart. We will always be friends and always share special memories of those glorious basketball days at Everett High School and Michigan State University back in the 1970s. I am anxious for you to read about those "magical moments" that were so special to both of us. This book will always hold a special place on my bookshelf at home.

For those of you who have been around Tim's work these many years—enjoy reminiscing what has been special to him. For those who have seen and heard Tim for just a brief period of time—then you'll have fun catching up with all that you have missed.

Earvin "Magic" Johnson

CHAPTER 1

Early Scoop

The 11 p.m. newscast had ended and another long work day was over. In November of 1972, I was single and I spent the majority of my time trying to become the best sportscaster I could. I was 23 years old and I had already spent 18 months as the lead sports anchor at the old WJIM-TV in Lansing.

Dinner hours were short and 12-hour workdays were typical. In those early years on the air, I anchored the sports news six days a week. There were no assistants and I had no other help. I was the lone sportscaster at the station. There was an 11 p.m. newscast on Saturdays—not an early 6 p.m. show as there is today. And the only Sunday news we carried was from CBS.

On this Thursday night I decided that the day still had a couple of hours to enjoy outside the studio. Our news producer at the time was another single friend of mine named John Join. He was a bit older and a talented guy and he had a bit more experience in the business than I had. He was very dedicated to quality work and because of that I enjoyed being around him. We decided that a beer together would be an appropriate way to end a productive day.

Less than a mile from the studio was a restaurant popular with the Michigan State coaches from various sports. It had a separate lounge area and often coaches and others close to the school's athletic programs would spend time together there after hours. I liked to stop there because I usually found some familiar company.

On this particular night, one of the Spartans' assistant football coaches was present and it was clear he had been there long before John and I arrived. I'll call him Bill because to this day I always promised him I would protect his identity. By the time last call was announced he had given me the best scoop I'd ever uncovered and to this day it is the biggest story I've ever broken.

The Spartan football team was having another difficult season. Duffy Daugherty's popularity as head coach was waning considerably since the glory days of the mid-1960s. The Spartans' record was 2-4-1 and their play had been sloppy the entire season. Duffy was in his 19th year and while many figured he would not coach much longer, no one really figured that this would be his last season.

Bill joined us for a beer and at one point he asked me, "When do you think Duffy will step down as head coach?" I told him I didn't know, but I didn't think he was ready to quit. After discussing the subject back and forth Bill looked me in the eye and said, "It's over. He's announcing his retirement after Saturday's game. He told the players and coaches about it yesterday and today."

I wasn't sure I was hearing him right. I pressed him— "Are you sure?" This was too big a story to hear without getting him to repeat it to me with more substantiation.

"Trust me, it's over," he reiterated. I could tell that this was an emotional moment for an assistant coach whose own future was suddenly up in the air now that his longtime boss was leaving. He needed someone to talk to and we had known each other for some time. Whether he told me about Duffy for the purpose of having me release it early is a question for which I never learned the answer.

After a sleepless night, I decided to track down a follow-up source. I called a couple of players I knew and tried to trap them into confirming what I had been told. Several played dumb, saying that they hadn't heard about it, but one finally bought my line and confirmed what I had been told the previous night—Duffy was announcing his retirement after Saturday's game effective at the end of the season.

That afternoon I told my boss, WJIM-TV owner Harold F. Gross, exactly what I had heard. He pressed me to make sure I had it right and I convinced him that the story was accurate. We decided to release the story at the top of the 6 p.m. news that Friday night, on the eve of the game against Purdue. We ran a "crawl" on the screen all during the afternoon which alerted viewers to the fact that we would break a "major sports story" at six o'clock.

In those days, Michigan State always hosted a little media party at the University Club for those gathering to cover the next day's game. Duffy always attended and I enjoyed being a part of the scene. I was always late to the party because I could never arrive until after the six o'clock news.

On this night some of the local sports writers were watching our newscast in the bar of the University Club. They had been tipped off that I was about to break a story and they wanted to see what it was. I came on the air and simply stated what I had heard—after 19 seasons Duffy Daugherty would announce his retirement as the Spartans' legendary coach following tomorrow's game with Purdue. I said I had a couple of good sources and that was it.

The moment I got off the air the phone began ringing in my office. The wire services had been alerted to the story by our staff and now it was making national sports headlines and I was being quoted. I was a bit nervous but I was also excited. This was big news and I had broken a big story. Other media were calling to quote me and get more details.

My next move was to head to the University Club for the media party since I knew I would have to face Duffy sooner or later. While I figured the encounter would not be pleasant, I never dreamed Duffy would be as upset as he was.

I never called Duffy to verify this story—all he would have done is deny it, try to talk me out of running it, or release it to someone else.

The moment the news aired, the 25 or so media people in attendance cornered Duffy when he arrived and told him about my comments. He was taken completely off guard and wasn't sure how to handle the situation. He eventually held a small, impromptu news conference and confirmed what I had said to be true. He literally broke down as the emotion of the moment and the finality of his long career got the best of him. He was escorted out of the room by longtime WJR radio sportscaster Bob Reynolds who got him to agree to a special interview which they would air that evening. As they were departing the room to go make their tape, I walked in the door.

"I hope your scoop was well worth it!," Duffy screamed. His

face was red and tears were in his eyes. I asked to speak to him for a moment, but Reynolds quickly led him away. I walked into the reception area and drank a beer to calm down, but there wasn't much reason for me to stick around. The rest of the media had fled to file their stories.

Later that evening, I heard Reynolds on the air with Duffy. He commented, "The young man will have to live with what he has done to you." The interview then shifted to Duffy's decision and Duffy calmed down a bit.

Had I uncovered this story today, I would have handled its follow up much better than I did 25 years ago. I was a bit intimidated by all the commotion and that night on the 11 p.m. news I actually apologized for my decision to break the story, though it was the purpose of my job in the first place.

Let me say that I hold no resentment toward Bob Reynolds over his comments about me in that interview. We are friends to this day. In those days, WJR radio had nothing to do with Michigan games. The station aired MSU football and Reynolds was the reason why. He was close to Michigan State and to Duffy. The story caught him off guard as it did many others and I think he was covering his tracks that night.

The late Bob Hoerner, former sports editor of the Lansing State Journal, also was caught without this story, but he defended me and was good to me through it all. For that I have always been grateful.

At the time of the incident, I had just begun a friendship with Joe Falls, columnist for the Detroit Free Press. In my defense, he wrote in his column that I was only doing my job and should not be blamed for upsetting Duffy's plan of waiting until after the game to make his announcement.

The Spartans beat Purdue 22-12 and went on to win three of their final four games. But that weekend was difficult for me because of all the fuss and commotion. On Sunday night I even went to Duffy's house, unannounced, to try and square matters with him. He was cordial, mostly because I think the emotion of the moment had passed and there was nothing further to be gained by beating on me. He clearly wanted to find out who had told me and to this day I think he always had an idea who it was. However, he couldn't prove it and after all, it made little difference at that point any way.

I truly believe that after this incident my relationship with Duffy changed forever. Whereas he had always been cordial to me before, he always seemed somewhat distant to me in the years I saw him up to his death in 1987. I never made an issue of it with him, but I always felt a chill around him. I don't think he ever trusted me from that point on and I feel bad about it because he was truly a hero to me growing up.

I begin this book with this story because it is one of the more vivid memories I have held over all these years. I don't think I have ever broken a story quite as big and I am the first to admit that it came my way out of sheer luck. I just happened to be in a lounge at a time when a well-oiled assistant coach was desperate to tell someone the big story he knew all about. Most big stories are broken through a bit of luck and this one was no different.

What helped on the Duffy story was the fact that there were far fewer media people covering MSU football in those days than there are today. In 1972, with the Spartans losing, there wasn't nearly as much attention paid to the team on a regular basis as there might otherwise have been. I didn't have to "beat" as many reporters as one has to today.

Little did I know that over 30 years, one of my most significant stories would occur so early in my career. There have been many more since then, but the days surrounding Duffy's resignation and my involvement with them are memories I will never forget.

C H A P T E R 2

Life Among The Spartans 1

I was born in March, 1949, in Bloomington, Indiana, and I never hesitate to remind Bobby Knight of this when I am looking for an advantage in getting an interview with him. My dad was working in the School of Business at Indiana University before accepting a faculty job at M.I.T. in suburban Boston. He then accepted a position on the faculty at Michigan State, where he would eventually become Chairman of the Department of Marketing and Transportation Administration. He worked at MSU from 1955 through 1968, situated in two different offices. I always enjoyed visiting him there. General Motors recruited him for several years and finally in January, 1969, he accepted a job as General Marketing manager for Chevrolet Division. My mother and my younger sister, Becky, moved with him to Birmingham and I was left to live among the Spartans on my own.

My parents bought a home in the Glencairn section of East Lansing which happened to be just a couple of doors down and across the street from legendary MSU football coach Duffy Daugherty. My parents became good friends with them and my mother was very close to Duffy's wife, Francie. The Daughertys lived in a middle-class home like we did—college football coaches salaries weren't nearly commensurate in the 1950s with what they are today.

The Daughertys had two children. Dan is a couple of years older than I am and his sister Dree was close in age with my own sister. Dan and I ran cross country together for a year at East Lansing High School. He never had an interest in playing football mainly because he did not have the physical size. Dan and I later shared an apartment at Michigan State for a year and he was intensely loyal to his father. The entire Daugherty family, for that matter, was very close-knit.

Duffy Daugherty was easily the biggest sports hero of my childhood. I idolized him. I well remember playing football in the street after school and each fall, at about six o'clock, Duffy would drive through our game en route home after practice. Often times he would get out of his car and hand deliver a couple of sideline passes to an upcoming Spartan game to my brother Greg and me. To say we were thrilled is putting it mildly.

Going to Michigan State football games while growing up was great. My first game was in 1958, a year after Spartan Stadium added the upper decks. I didn't see all of the home games—occasionally I was grounded for a variety of in-house offenses.

I tell my parents I never wanted for anything growing up. They made my life joyful to the point that I hope my own boys are as happy as I was—and having Duffy for a neighbor was icing on the cake.

I chose to attend Michigan State because I had part-time jobs in journalism that I figured I might not get at another school. I lived on campus, in McDonel Hall, my freshman and sophomore years. I worked part-time in the MSU sports information office for a year under Fred Stabley, Sr., one of the finest people I ever met. I became close friends with Fred and his long-time assistant Nick Vista and those two helped my career in more ways than I can ever count. Fred's son, Fred Junior, is a couple of years older than I am and has been a close personal friend of mine for years.

When Fred Sr. died on December 8, 1996, his son asked me to deliver the eulogy, something I had never done before. I spent hours writing it and rehearsing how I would deliver it. I was as nervous as I have ever been delivering a speech. The elder Stabley was easy to praise—and the writing skills he taught me when I'd worked in his office some 29 years earlier helped form the document I'd prepared for his funeral.

Duffy, Fred and Nick are just a few of the countless wonderful people I have known well over the years in my association with Michigan State.

When I had a paper route, athletic director Biggie Munn was one of my customers. He treated me nicely and often gave me great tickets to hockey games in the old Dem Hall. I was bat boy for the baseball teams of John Kobs for a couple of years in the early 1960s and even got my picture in the paper once congratulating one of the Spartans after he'd hit a home run. I got to make a couple of road trips to Michigan on the bus with the team and thought that was just about the greatest thing in the world.

I majored in journalism. My professors were very talented, though many of them thought sportswriting was a waste of time and effort. I took 54 out of 180 hours in journalism, the most I could get. I had some kind of job all the way through college and it took me four years and two summer terms to get my degree. I had a 2.85 grade point average on the 4.0 scale. I wasn't too interested in the core courses, but I loved the journalism and that's where I got good enough grades to finish with nearly a straight B average.

Since I attended my first MSU football game in 1958, that means I've spent some 40 years around MSU athletics. I've seen plenty of highs and lows. I've seen many people come and go. I've watched the school exhibit greatness and I've watched it struggle. I've spent hours on the campus in a variety of activities.

I loved the basketball games in Jenison Fieldhouse. In those days the capacity was 12,500 and the raised floor gave it a terrific look. I saw some great Spartan players—Johnny Green, Bob Anderegg, Stan Washington and Pete Gent to name a few.

A couple of moments stand out. The great Ohio State teams of 1960-62 dominated the entire Big Ten and in 1961 Jerry Lucas scored 48 points in Jenison, leading the Buckeyes to an 83-68 victory. The house was packed. Lucas was a fantastic college player. So was Michigan's Cazzie Russell and those teams put on a marvelous show.

No player in modern basketball had a game like Indiana guard Jimmy Rayl. The pint-sized gunner shot from anywhere—today they'd call him a ball hog. I watched him score more than 50 points on a couple of occasions. There was not the television coverage of the games then like there is today, so attending the games was a bigger deal than today's fans experience.

In 1963, when I was 14 years old, my parents gave me money to buy tickets to attend the NCAA Regionals in Jenison. In those days, only 16 teams made it to the NCAA tournament. There were four regionals of four teams each. Jenison hosted Illinois,

Bowling Green, Loyola of Chicago and Mississippi State.

Days before the tournament began, the big story was about Mississippi State. The Governor of Mississippi nearly prevented his team from attending because it would be competing against black players. The story confused me at the time. Finally the all-white Bulldog team made it to East Lansing and was eliminated. Imagine such a story today, 35 years later.

Gus Ganakas has always been a dear friend. He coached the Spartans for seven years after John Benington's untimely death in 1969, just prior to the start of the season. Biggie Munn had high respect for Gus and promptly promoted him from assistant to head coach. Gus had been a tremendous high school coach at East Lansing, leading his Trojans to the 1958 class B state title over vaunted River Rouge.

He arrived at MSU as the Ralph Young Fund Development Director. Shortly thereafter Benington talked him in to becoming an assistant. Benington was as classy a head coach as MSU has ever had in any sport. He and Gus were a perfect match.

Gus had a limited salary and a limited budget, but he had a winning record. In January, 1975, he suspended most of his team just prior to a game against rugged Indiana because of some insubordination at a morning meeting. In those days, schools had junior varsity teams and the Spartans had to quickly assemble a makeshift club from among the JV's with just a few hours notice. Indiana won 107-55 and after a tense weekend, the suspended players were reinstated. That team finished with a 17-9 record, but the episode was the beginning of the end for Gus as head coach.

He was reassigned in the athletic department a season later when the Spartans fired football coach Denny Stolz over the lengthy NCAA investigation. MSU President Clifton Wharton called Gus to a Sunday afternoon meeting after the 1976 season in which the Spartans finished with a 14-13 record. Gus thought he was going to get a raise. His friends tease him about that incident to this day.

Gus's dismissal nearly cost Michigan State getting Earvin Johnson. Gus had done a superb job recruiting Earvin and the two became friends throughout Earvin's early high school years. Earvin was upset when Gus was let go and that's what began the recruiting uncertainty for him as to whether he really wanted to play for the Spartans.

Gus Ganakas is one of the greatest ambassadors Michigan State has ever had. Every where he goes, people love to visit with him because of his warm demeanor and sense of humor. Veteran coaches at other schools love Gus, especially Bobby Knight, who goes out of his way to see him every time the Spartans and Hoosiers meet during the winter.

Gus is now working for Tom Izzo full-time in the basketball office and even though he has passed his 70th birthday, he is still a great asset to the school. Had Gus been able to perhaps corral his players a bit more when he was coaching who knows how great his teams with Earvin might have been. It is to Gus's credit that when Jud Heathcote replaced him he quickly made a friend-ship with his successor. Jud always appreciated Gus for that and the two remain good friends to this day. Whatever bitterness Gus felt over his dismissal, after a winning season no less, he largely kept it to himself and tried to fit into the athletic department in his new role. I don't know one person who doesn't have high regard for Gus.

I got to know all the school presidents. All the praise John Hannah received through the years was richly deserved. His lead-ership is rare. After he retired I saw him at a football game and he told me, "I watch your show—I don't always agree with what you say, but I watch."

I would have loved to sit down with him to find out where he disagreed with me. One of John's sons, Dave, was a year ahead of me at East Lansing High School and we ran cross country together.

When Hannah left Michigan State, it spelled the beginning of the end for Duffy, who never felt he got even close to the same support from the new president, Clifton Wharton.

Duffy received several job offers during his MSU years, the best of which was from Notre Dame. Dr. Hannah talked Duffy into staying at in East Lansing, but I'll bet Duffy might have done it over differently if he knew how his career would play itself out. Duffy's personality and Irish background would have played famously in South Bend working for the famed Father Theodore Hesburgh, the Notre Dame president. Hannah was the main rea-son Duffy stayed and when Hannah retired in 1969, Duffy's career would never recover from the few down years he was experiencing.

Wharton had little experience in college athletics. He was a bright man, but the reality of dealing with big-time sports was a mystery to him. I felt he mishandled the vast NCAA investigation into MSU's football program. He personally handled much of the probe and after fighting with the NCAA, he got rid of Duffy's successor, Denny Stolz, along with athletic director Burt Smith and of course, Gus. Michigan State got an enormous three-year probation and it took years to recover from that penalty.

Cecil Mackey served as President for a few years and I probably mistreated him worse than anyone I've ever dealt with in my career. Mackey is still on the faculty at Michigan State and he couldn't be nicer to me when I see him. I am ashamed about the way I handled some of his problems involving athletics. I didn't always agree with him, but I probably did a very poor job communicating with him. He knows college sports very well.

John DiBiaggio was also a bright guy. He was also very stubborn and he let his problems with George Perles literally cost him his presidency. How foolish. DiBiaggio simply could not find any room for compromise with Perles over George's dual role of football coach and athletic director. George, of course, was just as stubborn and neither one of them are with MSU anymore. I have long felt that had they had a mutual trust and a close working relationship that they could have gone down as heroes in the history of the school. George would have become full-time athletic director and he would have been tremendous in that single role. But when the president struggles with the football coach and vice versa, both are headed for a fall. What a waste of two talented people.

Peter McPherson has given MSU some stability. He has had to learn the ropes about college sports along the way, but he has a close rapport with the coaches.

I thought all the interim presidents did superb jobs. Walter Adams, the late Dr. Edgar Harden and Gordon Guyer all were loyal Spartans who demonstrated excellent people skills. All were respected. Guyer is one of the most brilliant guys I've met in a long time. He is a masterful ad lib speaker. People like him and had he wanted to remain as the MSU president, I think he would have gone down as one of the school's all-time great contributors. But he didn't want the hassle of the job and said so the moment he was appointed to the interim post.

Michigan State has one of the greatest campuses in the world and its diversity of students make it truly a special place. The school's sports fans flock in big numbers to the games when the teams have even the slightest morsel of success. The hockey sell-outs are now legendary and the football and basketball attendance is good when the team is competitive.

In my judgment, what has plagued MSU over the years is too many transitional people moving on and too many people involved with key decisions. For athletics to reach their full potential, I believe the president (of any major school) must have a rock solid athletic director and give him almost total control of the department. The two must have a close relationship and mutual trust. The athletic director must have power to hire and fire coaches, much the way Andy Geiger does at Ohio State. The president and athletic director alone should make the key decisions affecting the athletic programs. When too many others get involved, a smooth and orderly process is compromised. In turn, these two must then have a similar trusting relationship with the various head coaches. When all are united, then success has a paramount chance of following. Anything less than that and the job becomes considerably more difficult.

DiBiaggio's handling of the Perles situation regarding the athletic directorship was a crippling blow. He brought in a woman, Merrily Dean Baker, to serve as George's boss, knowing full well that this set up would never work. John did not have Michigan State's best interests at heart, in my judgment.

Several weeks after Baker came aboard, DiBiaggio left for Tufts University and Merrily had no chance to succeed. I always got along with her and I actually felt sorry for the impossible situation in which she was placed. The MSU athletic director's job would be difficult for any woman because gaining credibility with so many males would be a big obstacle. She would be dealing with individuals who have a pre-prejudice about gender—imagine all those males allowing a woman to go out and hire a head football or basketball coach. Merrily had no chance to hold that kind of authority. An athletic director without that level of responsibility is an athletic director in title only, the way I see it.

She struck a good financial deal to leave MSU and she did not take the low road in doing it. She kept her mouth shut about the agony she endured in her short term at MSU, but the debacle may well have cost her a continuing career in college sports. As I write this she is still not employed in a similar college job.

Michigan State has seemingly always struggled to find a comfortable fit for its athletic director. Even Biggie Munn had some rough times. Here was a guy who actually hired Duffy Daugherty as an assistant football coach. He recommended his promotion. Wouldn't you think that groundwork alone would set the stage for a superb one-two combination between the two? It absolutely did not. The two had strong egos and only the intervention by President Hannah kept their relationship from deteriorating totally. Hannah put Duffy in charge of the "football department" and Biggie was athletic director of everything else. It was hardly the best arrangement, but it settled matters until one of them moved on.

Biggie's successor, Burt Smith, had little authority. When he tried to hire a football coach, he ran into plenty of roadblocks.

Joe Kearney may have been the best athletic director the Spartans have had since I've been around. He had good people skills and plenty of broad experience. He was a likable guy and he had the authority to hire coaches. He brought in Darryl Rogers and Jud Heathcote and had little interference with both appointments.

Had Kearney and Rogers stayed on longer than they did, Michigan State might have had a much more successful decade in the 1980s.

Kearney was nervous about the arrival of Cecil Mackey as the school's new president. When a chance to go to Arizona State as athletic director arose, he jumped at it. He took Darryl with him and there were many bad feelings left behind in East Lansing.

As it turned out, Kearney's move was probably wise in that it led to his ultimate desired position as Commissioner of the Western Athletic Conference. Darryl stayed at Arizona State a short while then moved on to an ill-fated appointment with the Detroit Lions. Now he is out of coaching.

Darryl is a terrific person. He is friendly and fun to be around. He did not have a "prima donna" aura that afflicts so many big-time head coaches. He had a wide open offense that the fans loved and all the players liked his laid back personality.

Recruiting became a problem because rival coaches constantly advised prospective players that Darryl would soon leave Michigan State for the NFL. The rumors wore Darryl down and being a west coast guy in the first place, the Arizona State move seemed too good to pass up at the time.

My relationship with Doug Weaver was somewhat rocky. He became Michigan State's athletic director after Kearney left and he was given a great deal of authority. He put the athletic department on solid financial footing, but some of that was at the expense of the so-called non-revenue sports, most of which struggled during the 1980s.

Doug and I are cordial today, but it wasn't always that way. In 1981, he banned me from doing the play-by-play of MSU basketball. What a hassle.

There was no Big Ten network in those days. A private company won the rights to MSU basketball, but the school had the right of announcer approval. Never mind the fact that I had broadcast the games for several years previous and that I got along well with Jud Heathcote. Doug thought I was too controversial with regards to the university. So he wanted someone else to work the games.

When his decision was made it made news across the state. I was upset and surprised. Several area prominent attorneys phoned and offered their assistance on my behalf free of charge. I actually sent one attorney to go visit with the MSU counsel with the hope of being reinstated. Jud was against my ouster because he thought I would become a martyr and the situation would get too much adverse publicity. I was advised of my options and a lawsuit became a distinct possibility. I was being denied my right to pursue my livelihood. Here I was offered a play-by-play job and the university was denying me of that opportunity on the grounds I was "controversial." I was not about to slant the news just so I could stay in favor with someone who had the right to terminate my play-by-play work.

In hindsight, there were issues that I discussed on television that I overdid in those days. Commentaries were a big part of sportscasts in the 1980s and I enjoyed writing and delivering them. I only commented on local issues and of course, MSU was the biggest player on the local scene. Doug Weaver did not like all the things I said on the air, though he rarely discussed with me what bothered him.

The late Burt Smith gained my respect because he would always phone me to address problems with me. If he didn't like something I said, he would call me and we'd talk it out. More often than not he convinced me that there were other sides to an issue I'd comment on and my stance would change. At least what he told others about me, he also told me directly over the phone. I admired him for that.

I was debating whether to file suit against MSU when I got a memorable phone call from Joe Falls of the Detroit News. He advised against it. He suggested that working games under a court order and filing suit against Michigan State was not in my best interests. I quickly concluded he was right, so I let the matter pass.

After the season ended, Doug called me and we went for a ride in his old van around campus. Doug told me he was willing to start over with our relationship and I could work the games in the future. I told him I would not alter my style just to regain my job, but I appreciated his change of heart and the issue ended with that meeting.

Doug was always uncomfortable being interviewed, certainly with me anyway. He would almost never do a spur of the moment session, which I do with many subjects today. He wanted them set up in advance and he always wanted to know the subject matter. Controversial topics did not make him happy to cooperate and he was hard to pin down for information.

However, when I needed some MSU items donated for charity activities, Doug was very helpful. And when I was the subject of a "roast" for another charity fund-raiser, Doug agreed to be a speaker and he was very funny. I appreciated his participation because I knew I was not one of his favorite people.

The pressures of the job got to him a bit and he decided to retire with his health intact. His wife Nancy was struggling with her own well-being and the time seemed right for him. Doug owned a summer home in northern Michigan where he would spend time with George Perles, Jud Heathcote and Ron Mason. It is to his credit that he became close friends with them, all of them working on the same page. I have long felt that in any business, all the employees must be working together, with the same goals, and all must strive to help each other. It is hard enough to succeed in a highly competitive atmosphere. When the troops are fighting amongst themselves how can they battle the enemy?

Doug hired two football coaches in his tenure, Muddy Waters and George Perles. Everyone thought Perles would get the job and was the perfect choice, when Waters was hired. I remember standing in the old WJIM-TV newsroom in 1980 when Muddy's announcement came over the wire service machine.

There had been speculation about Darryl Rogers' successor for weeks. Many names were tossed about but no one mentioned Hillsdale's Muddy Waters. I was dumbfounded when I heard the news—I couldn't believe with all the big names available for this major job that anyone would hire a small college coach in his late 50s. On the air that same night, I said in a commentary "they blew it." In hindsight, I'm not very proud of condemning Muddy before he even arrived on the scene, but I felt all along that his chances at success would be limited.

Muddy was fired after three years and a 10-23 record. Attendance was down, the natives were restless and Doug was forced into a move possibly to save his own career at the same time.

Muddy was too good a person to be subjected to the sometimes dirty business of major college football. He had many strikes against him. His staff of assistants was assembled in haste and he perhaps didn't have the best available coaches to work with him. He lost many close games that could have gone either way.

Muddy never held my negativism against me and even asked me to host his television show. We usually taped it after home games in the locker room and that wasn't very pleasant most of the time because the Spartans usually had just lost. He never came close in three tries against Michigan and it was only a matter of time before he would be replaced.

Muddy didn't hold grudges and he didn't let the criticism overwhelm him. He loved Michigan State and he believed in the basic goodness of all human beings. He was a very upbeat guy in an often negative business. He did not become bitter after his dismissal and tried to help his successor, Perles.

I never got the feeling that George was the guy Doug Weaver ever wanted as the Spartans' head coach. He did not hire him the first time around of course and I remember visiting with George on the phone in Pittsburgh trying to help him land the job. In fact, I had to deliver the news to George's wife Sally, on the phone, when the announcement about Muddy was made. She struggled to hold her emotions in check.

George played his cards right after Waters was hired. He didn't run his mouth, so he stayed in favor with the Michigan State people. His stock as a potential head coach rose the more Muddy lost. Weaver knew that Perles would be a popular successor, so they quickly made a deal to bring George to East Lansing.

But even that got botched. George was under contract to the U.S. Football League's Philadelphia Stars, to whom he had recently signed a contract. The process of asking for permission to interview him for the MSU job was not up to the standards expected by Stars' owner Myles Tanenbaum. He nailed MSU for a $175,000 contract settlement and the legal fees included pushed the entire investment to land Perles more than that.

This is no kidding—I was the most impressed with George Perles the first day he walked on to campus at his introductory news conference in December, 1982. The media had assembled at the Kellogg Center for an early afternoon session and George was on top of his game. He looked and sounded great. Coming off three straight losing football seasons, he knew what to say to win the frustrated Spartan fans over. I was even ready to suit up and play for him after hearing him that day. He was well-organized and prepared for all the questions he received.

The family I have today is the result of my relationship with George Perles. Soon after he was named the MSU coach, I was in the running to host his television show in the fall. When that did not work out he asked me what he could do to make up for my disappointment. I casually suggested, "How about four tickets on the 50 for the Notre Dame game?"

I didn't think about the request after that but sure enough he sent me four good tickets for the second game of season in late September, 1983, in South Bend.

I asked my attorney to get a date and join me and my date for a day of fun. My luck wasn't too good at that time. My companion called the morning of the game to tell me she couldn't go. "Severe menstrual cramps" was her reason.

I had no time to find a replacement so off the three of us went on a gorgeous day with a big cooler joining me in the back seat.

Our one female in the threesome was Cathy Kearns, an MSU grad who taught elementary school in Brighton. She was 30 years old, never been married and owned her own house in Farmington

Hills. Since she was seated in the middle at the game we had plenty of time to talk. She didn't know anything about me and wasn't at all impressed about who I was or what I did for a living.

The day was quite eventful. Gerry Faust's Fighting Irish pushed the Spartans all over the field, but somehow lost 28-23 because MSU quarterback Dave Yarema made just enough big plays for the Spartans to leave town with an upset victory. George was 2-0 at that point in his first season and the locals were getting mighty excited.

Cathy and her date were just good friends—they had known each other for years. He suggested that I call her sometime just to say hi. The following weekend I flew to San Diego to visit another female I was seeing at the time. I knew on the way home I was going to call Cathy Kearns and ask her out.

We started going out and even went to church together early on. She was and is a devout Catholic and I was and am a devout Missouri Synod Lutheran. By December we were engaged. We married on June 30, 1984, less than nine months after George Perles gave me those tickets. I probably never would have met her if I'd been the host of the first Perles television show.

We've been married for 14 years and have three boys and at this time, they are all healthy. George doesn't openly take credit for my good family fortune, but facts are facts. Because of him I have a family to love, depend on and enjoy. Even if you always did run the ball on first down, I owe you one, George. How can I ever thank you?

CHAPTER 3

Life Among The Spartans 2

The many George Perles controversies have been well-documented over the years. Somehow problems just seemed to follow him year after year, for a variety of different reasons. George was about as stubborn a coach as I'd ever met in terms of strategy. He once told me, "If you are going to run the ball, you better win, brother!" As you all know, George ran the ball and ran the ball—left, right and up the middle.

I am absolutely convinced that the turning point in his Michigan State career came at the Rose Bowl after the 1987 season. Up to that point he had not brought Michigan State to the top of the mountain. He was still completely focused on winning and getting to Pasadena. Nothing interfered with his determination. The 1987 team improved as the year went along after getting crushed early in the season by Notre Dame and Florida State.

George has always loved the good life and parties and people and friends. His experience at the Rose Bowl had to be one of the true highlights of his life. When the Spartans edged Southern Cal 20-17 he was on top of the Spartans' world. But it was at that point, in my estimation, that his tenure in East Lansing began a downhill run.

There was conjecture about his leaving for an NFL head coaching job and George did little to stop the various rumors and reports. He positioned himself for the now infamous ten-year contract. He was smart enough to land job security with essentially one championship season. He was frankly more shrewd than the people he was dealing with. I was happy for George when he got the long-term deal but thought it was not in Michigan State's best interests. To me that contract sent a message that the school could not possibly afford to lose him. He was the one hope to win football games and no one else could come in and lead the Spartans to the Rose Bowl. During that championship season, George had what appeared to be a solid relationship with President John DiBiaggio. But it was all about to crumble to the point where they would end up knocking each other out of Michigan State.

The crisis reached a crescendo when Doug Weaver stepped down as athletic director. George and Doug were close friends. When George Perles is your friend, you indeed have one heckuva friend. George is very loyal. He was loyal as can be to Doug Weaver. Working for someone other than Doug made him extremely nervous.

So the answer was to become both athletic director and head coach, just like Bo Schembechler did for a time at Michigan and like Joe Paterno did for a time at Penn State. George would handle both jobs for a couple of years, then choose his successor as football coach and finish his professional career as the MSU athletic director. He had his game plan all mapped out.

DiBiaggio was never convinced that George should handle both jobs. He felt that Perles would be answering only to himself with no checks and balances within the athletic department. His argument was based on his own principles, and he had a good point.

It is well-documented how George eventually landed the dual role with intervention from the board of trustees, much to DiBiaggio's dismay. I thought it was embarrassing the way the two of them went at it. They absolutely could not find any common ground in their dispute. The feud also divided the MSU camp. George was determined to succeed as athletic director, but that came at a cost to his football coaching. He might deny it to this day, but the dual role caused him to shift his focus. All you have to do is look at the Spartans' records after George took on the additional duties.

To me, compromise could have been achieved. George could have been given the dual role with DiBiaggio's blessing under a framework whereby he directly answered to the administration on a regular basis. I thought that could be worked out. DiBiaggio had to know that George was planning to get out of coaching and they probably could have agreed on a suitable timetable. By then, egos got involved and it was only a matter of time before they were both gone.

I liked John, but he lost me over this. Here was a guy who was hugging Perles after the Spartans clinched their Rose Bowl bid in 1987. Why would anyone lose a presidency, which he loved, because of a stubborn football coach?

George was equally to blame. I always felt that he needed a wise friend he could trust over his tenure at MSU who would give him sound advice. George had plenty of influential and political friends. But most told him what he wanted to hear or didn't offer the proper advice to get him out of his jams.

He would have been much better off to make his peace with DiBiaggio and not pursue the dual role. A coach must have a solid rapport with his president—no exceptions. Perhaps he could have played a role in choosing a successor to Weaver, someone he could have worked with. We shall never know.

If George was stubborn, he was also determined. He was going to show everyone he had talent as an athletic director—and truly he did. He had a sensitivity for the problems of all the coaches in the department and they appreciated that. He was creative. Most of his staff was very loyal to him. He would have had a gangbuster's career as an athletic director, but for one problem— he had absolutely no working relationship with the school president. It was that way not only with DiBiaggio, but also his successor, Peter McPherson. It would turn out to be a fatal flaw.

I was present the moment George met McPherson for the first time. It was at Picture Day in August, 1993, and McPherson had just been named the school's president. Peter was brought to the stadium and he and George posed for photographers after some polite opening greetings. George immediately invited McPherson to go with the team to Japan for the season's final game against Wisconsin. George had set that game up through representatives of Coca-Cola and he managed to arrange it without losing a home game. He got Wisconsin to give up a game in Madison, ironically because Wisconsin's attendance had suffered through losing seasons. Coincidentally, it was in Japan that the Badgers clobbered the Spartans to win a trip to the Rose Bowl.

The Spartans struggled in '93 and again in '94, and on several occasions McPherson contemplated dumping Perles as coach. He was always persuaded to wait, but when the NCAA probe was ready to be launched in '94, McPherson made his move.

George's popularity with the fans was gone and attendance was down. The Spartans were losers and years of controversies finally caught up with him. The president did not wait until the end of the season. The announcement came with two games to go and it was an awkward mess all the way around.

Settling George's contract was another hassle which took several more years to sort out. He filed suit at one point, then quickly retracted it.

George Perles is much brighter than he sometimes comes across to people, because public speaking was not his specialty. When he is resolved to be successful at any given project there is no stopping him.

His work with the local Special Olympics has indeed been something special. He has raised hundreds of thousands of dollars each August with his golf outing and he has spent a great deal of time making sure that it would be successful. His motivation was launched because of the son of one of his assistant coaches. His friend and longtime assistant Norm Parker had a boy active in Special Olympics. George got involved because he was touched by the plight afflicting that one child.

I was astounded how he founded the Motor City Bowl. At the time he went to prospective sponsors, his name was not exactly number one on people's popularity lists. But he doggedly pursued Ford Motor Company and convinced its people to sign a multi-million dollar five-year contract to host a bowl game involving the Mid-American Conference. He added friends of his to key staff positions who were struggling on their own. Ken Hoffman was pushed out as MSU's sports information director, but he was a close friend of George's. Perles made him a big part of the Motor City Bowl and took him to Hawaii with him to work on the Hula Bowl, where George also had an interest. His retired long-time secretary, Mary Kay Smith, was also given a Motor City Bowl job.

I saw Mary Kay at the Detroit airport last spring. I was going to a Big Ten basketball telecast in Minneapolis and she was going to Florida for six weeks. We bumped into each other and George's name came up.

"If any of George's friends called him from anywhere in the world with a problem, he'd find a way to help that person out," Mary Kay told me. I couldn't have agreed with her more.

George and I had a few run-ins over his coaching tenure. My goodness, how could we not, considering all the controversies I had to report. What I admired, though, was that when we would go at it hot and heavy on the phone we would always end the conversation cordially. You could argue with George and he would listen to you.

Near the end of his coaching tenure, he paged me off the golf course one afternoon in August. The night before, I read a story on my late sportscast about a line in Sports Illustrated. It was from the magazine's college preview issue. It said something to the affect that MSU "had the most boring offense in America."

I edited down the copy because of time constraints and George didn't like it. He screamed at me about not reading all of the story verbatim.

"Did you drag me off the golf course just to tell me that?" I screamed back. I was in the Country Club of Lansing locker room with others around, listening to this. Finally we both cooled off and that was the last run-in I ever had with him.

Later, PASS television asked us to broadcast two MSU football games together in 1995, Nick Saban's first year as head coach. Our debut would be the Michigan game in East Lansing. George and I chatted briefly on the phone and agreed to meet on the day of the game, several hours early in the morning. We would feel each other out as to how we would work together.

As usual, George was fully prepared because he wanted to do well. He had charts and graphs and notes and he was excited about his opportunity. He wanted to stay in the game somehow and broadcasting was one alternative for former coaches. He thought if he did well on these cable assignments, he might get a chance with a larger network.

The game turned out to be one of the most exciting MSU-Michigan games of all time. The Spartans rallied in the final moments behind George's recruited quarterback, Tony Banks, to pull out a narrow victory. I watched George closely that day to check out his emotions. Would he want Michigan State to win? After all, these were essentially all players he had recruited and his former assistant was now their head coach. But I was fully convinced he was happy and excited that the Spartans won and I detected no trace of bitterness over his fate.

The next week we were sent to Indiana on a bitterly cold,

snowy day. We were high up in an open-air press box and I about froze to death. I left the TV lights on while we worked just to get some heat. The weather didn't bother the old coach. He worked with no overcoat, no sport coat, just a shirt and tie. He said his body fat would keep him warm and apparently it did. He never complained about the freezing temperatures once.

In my judgment, there were two key reasons why George did not go down as one of Michigan State's top coaches and/or athletic directors. One, he could not alter his basic belief in conservative football. He was not a contemporary college coach. I think he recruited well enough and when his Rose Bowl team won games, it was simply because it had better players. Secondly, he just could not find a close working relationship with two presidents. Had he have been able to, he might well be athletic director today and one of the best in America.

George has many good traits even though they were always overshadowed to the public by the problems I just mentioned. His life will be better off away from Michigan State even though I truly believe he loves the place as much as he has always said.

CHAPTER 4

Why Do They Do It?

One morning in December of 1970, I was sitting in a classroom in Michigan State's Jenison Fieldhouse. Never let it be said I was not a serious college student. This was class number 329—"Basketball Strategy." It was worth three credits and it was great if you wanted autographs—many MSU varsity athletes from various teams were my fellow classmates.

The instructor was Bob Nordmann, who also happened to serve the university as the top assistant to head coach Gus Ganakas. It would be a long day for him since that night the Spartans would play a home game. Nordmann's message that morning on the chalkboard was to outline his team's strategies.

I was moderately interested in the class—about as much as most of the other students. I ended up getting a 3.0 (a B) at the end of the term. My biggest problem with that class was trying to convince my father that this was a worthwhile course for my college curriculum.

Just imagine an assistant basketball coach at the major college level teaching a course today. It just doesn't happen any more. Even Jud Heathcote taught some basketball classes early in his career.

"The pressure on college coaches today is far greater than when I was doing it," Gus says. Gus ran the program from 1969-76.

I've been around all kinds of coaches over the years and Gus is absolutely right. There is no comparison to the pressures and time demands that coaches at the Big Ten level have today compared with their counterparts of even ten years ago.

One reason is salaries. Imagine the University of Florida paying its football coach, Steve Spurrier, $2 million per year, no matter how many games the Gators win. At Michigan State, Nick Saban earns $650,000 per year which is provided from several sources. Tom Izzo is in the $600,000 range. But these jobs are far from easy. The time demands are withering. I often wonder why more coaches do not suffer from burnout.

Duffy Daugherty coached at Michigan State 25 years prematurely. Had he been around in today's market, with his personality and successful record, his income would have been dramatically higher than it was when he retired in 1972—and that's even figuring inflation into it.

George Perles was intent upon making as much money as he could when he coached—but only so he could leave it for his family members. Jud Heathcote never cared too much one way or another about the level of income he could achieve. Because of that attitude, Jud never made as much money as he could have— with his speech-making ability alone, an agent could have garnered big dollars for him from appearances all over the country. Jud was more interested in spending his free time doing things he enjoyed.

I flew home with the MSU team one night after a game at Penn State during Tom Izzo's first year as the Spartans' head coach. Michigan State had just lost a tough 54-50 battle and Izzo slumped into the back of the team's small charter plane.

"I don't care about making money," he said to no one in particular. "I'm just a guy from the Upper Peninsula—all I want to do is win games."

The big time coaching mentality has changed somewhat over the years. The coaches can indeed earn some big money, but it all goes away if they're fired. And many coaches don't get much time to turn programs around. If the seats aren't filled, the coaches' job is in jeopardy.

Muddy Waters might have been given a little more time than three years to turn around MSU's football fortunes but for one problem—the fans were staying away from Spartan Stadium. His ouster was more an economic move than anything else. Even Perles' dismissal was somewhat dictated by faltering attendance.

On several occasions during the 97-98 season, I sat down with Izzo behind closed doors in his office just to chat as friends. We'd discuss a variety of topics, mostly personal. Tom occasionally asks my advice and I only have one central piece of it for him— be careful of burnout!

I don't know how he stood up physically, let alone emotionally, that season. It does not begin with practice on October 15th, which, by the way, I think is ridiculously too early. I saw him on the sidelines earlier in the fall at Spartan Stadium courting visiting recruits. All of those weekends were shot in terms of getting away with the family.

The games begin in early November. And when the Spartans began winning during the Big Ten portion of the schedule, the pressures began to mount to keep the momentum going.

"I'm not sure if there's more pressure on you when you're in first place or if you're in last place," he jokingly observed to me one day. "All I know is I don't want to find out."

Unlike football, basketball coaches do not generally get a week between games. They get a few days, at best. There is no time to celebrate or relax after a big win. Another game beckons in a couple of days. And that goes on and on through the winter. Then come the tournaments and now the Big Ten has added its own post season before the NCAA tournament unfolds. It isn't just March Madness, it's 12 months of madness.

I'd listen to Tom tape his coaches show with a gravelly voice from yelling during practices and games. He looked tired to me much of the time. He made speeches to booster clubs and other groups in the area. He'd get away to watch high school recruits play whenever he could.

He spent four endless days in February dealing with the Mateen Cleaves/Andre Hutson arrests.

I told Tom about my theories of longevity. I used his former boss, Jud Heathcote, as an example.

"Jud knew this job was a marathon, not a sprint," I pointed out. "He learned how to work hard and then get away from it to refresh his batteries. His assistant coaches, of course, had to work very hard, but they helped keep him physically and mentally fit to coach until he was nearly 70. He must have done something right in that regard."

I fear for most big time coaches suffering from burnout. The stress is constant. The thought process seems to be: If I'm not doing something regarding my job today, then I fall behind the other coaches in the league who likely are working.

There are demands to graduate players and to keep them out of trouble. Coaches must also make a variety of appearances, but their biggest obstacle, of course, is winning. They might win one game, but what about the next? They might win one year, but what about next season? Recruiting is relentless and one big catch means keeping a kid away from agents. It means taking that player and winning most of the time. The coach better keep the stands filled and the prices of tickets haven't gone down the last time I checked.

And those are just some of the problems for head coaches. It's somewhat worse for the assistants. I have never understood what is fun about being an assistant coach at the big time level—in virtually any sport.

At least the head coach makes the big money. At least the head coach gets the glory for the winning. At least he is the boss of the program and can delegate authority. None of that goes to the assistant coaches.

They lead a nomad life. They switch jobs almost constantly. Their families can never put down roots. Their income is limited. They are often on the road recruiting. And when assistant coaches land top notch high school players, it is the head coach who gets the credit as being a "good recruiter." If assistant coaches don't land good recruits, they are scolded for it if not fired. Love of the game is one thing—being a big time assistant coach is something else again. The motivation for many is to eventually become a head coach, but the vast majority never get their shot.

As much as I enjoy sports I've always surmised that I could never be a big time head coach. The losing is something I just could not take. Imagine being a head football coach. He absolutely spends night and day during the season preparing for the games. When he loses, every single thing he did the previous week in preparation had essentially been wasted time.

Like George Perles always said: "When you win, whatever you did was right. When you lose, whatever you did was wrong."

I could take the losing as an athlete in high school. I knew it wasn't all my fault and I knew that my entire life didn't depend on the success of that particular season. I had other interests and other priorities. But the success of the team means everything in the life of head coaches at the collegiate level.

Many of them do burn out and move on to other pursuits. For some of them, getting out of coaching is the best thing that ever happened to them.

Howard Weyers was an assistant at MSU to head football coach Denny Stolz. Howard was a very sharp guy and an aggressive recruiter. He was a central figure in the NCAA investigation of the Spartans' program in the mid-1970's. It resulted in him losing his job. He got out of coaching, entered private business and became very successful.

Some coaches who are fired several times over stay with it because they really don't know anything else. I think that's sad. There sure is more to life than putting up with the demands and pressures of coaching when all it produces is losing and getting fired.

For Lloyd Carr, 1997 was worth all the sweat and stress the Michigan football coach had to endure in his career. He didn't even know if he could take another year of that pressure after the 1996 season produced a 9-4 record. He went to Bo Schembechler for advice. Bo survived 21 years at Michigan. He must know something. Bo told him to focus on doing his best and to not pay any attention to all of the outside critics.

But if the Wolverines struggle in 1998, Lloyd Carr will get all the blame and whatever he achieved in '97 will mean almost nothing. Coaching is a "what have you done lately?" business.

The money that big time coaches make infuriates many within the university structure. They don't understand why coaches make more than the school president or anyone else on the payroll for that matter. I used to think that way too. But over the years, as I've watched the demands on these people, I don't believe most of them are overpaid at all. They can get fired and all the money disappears because of one bad season. No one else in a university has to win like the head coaches in the revenue sports must do.

Tom Izzo became a much more sought after "celebrity" after the 1998 season for winning several national coach of the year awards. He paid for his success during the season by having precious little time to himself and his family. He tried to accept as many speaking and appearance engagements as he could, most without compensation. Almost no request was too small for him. Hence, a quiet off-season was anything but.

Only in the Ivy League has the growth of big time sports been curtailed. The Ivy League is division one in basketball and hockey but the schools don't give athletic scholarships. The coaches don't make as much money, of course, as others in their profession, but then the demands on their winning and losing aren't quite the same either.

In an era when college sports have exploded with financial growth, the Ivy League is the last holdout for varsity athletics to be restricted within the academic framework of the various schools.

As you read this, no matter what time of day it is, consider where any of the football or basketball coaches at Michigan State are at this very moment. They most likely are not on vacation, nor are they mowing the lawn at home. They likely are not out shopping with family nor coaching one of their kids' teams. They probably aren't laying around the house reading a novel or outside painting the porch.

They are probably involved in some aspect of their job—after all if they aren't working, they know their competition probably is—and the chances of winning decrease.

C H A P T E R 5

Four Suggestions

Eric Hess is a key member of our staff at WILX-TV and a good friend. Besides playing golf together, we've been co-workers for several years. Eric, in my estimation, could be the lead sports anchor at any station in the market and I would hate to have to work against him. He has fine talent. Our competition made a mistake letting us hire him away.

He always teases me about the various aspects of Michigan State sports that bug me and until they are changed will drive me nuts until the day I die. Therefore, here are four suggestions for MSU I offer from living amongst the Spartans over the past 43 years:

1) The next time the football field needs replacing, use real grass. Use grass developed by MSU researchers who provide their sod to sports stadiums around the world. Michigan State needs to emphasize what it does well, and MSU is world-renowned for developing superb athletic grass. Explain to me, therefore, why Spartan Stadium has artificial turf. One of its officials told me once, "It's because we need the field for too many other activities." Baloney.

I'd put up the biggest sign I could outside the tunnel entrance: "Welcome—You are about to enter a stadium which houses the finest athletic turf grass ever developed—by researchers at Michigan State University."

Or words to that effect. If I have to explain the logic of this further I will never be able to convince you.

2) Add the luxury suites in Munn Arena immediately. They

could easily be pre-sold. Don't skimp on them, either. Make them as nice as possible. Add as many as the building will allow. This should free up some season tickets which can be sold to people who have been waiting patiently for years for a chance to buy them. Michigan State hockey will likely always be competitive. This is a win-win proposition. More seats made available will add more fans to a building that is always accused of being too quiet. Even with luxury suites, there will be a demand for tickets for MSU hockey games.

3) Pave the intramural field between the Breslin Center, Munn Arena, and the Ralph Young Track. Like Eric Hess says to me, "You just can't get past that can you?"

No Eric, I can't. If they ever pave it, bury me somewhere on the site.

They took out those awful tennis courts south of Spartan Stadium and added more parking and landscaped it beautifully. It can hardly be called an eyesore and now more fans have better parking. If they paved that intramural field it would create a great deal more convenient parking places for beleaguered fans who struggle to attend games in poor weather. The spaces could all be pre-sold. It could be landscaped. They could even put some basketball hoops around the pavement. The intramural fields could be moved to the southern portion of campus. While they're at it, put in some more parking spaces at the Breslin Center. Those broad sidewalks and all that grass is not necessary—it just makes it longer for fans to walk into the building in poor weather. I like Indiana—the basketball arena and the football stadium are adjacent each other. All of the land surrounding those facilities is used for parking and nothing else.

4) Quit playing baseball in February and March! This is not a problem for just Michigan State, but also for other northern schools. It makes no sense to play a summer game in the winter. They play these games in horrible weather—it's tough on the players and very few fans will brave the elements to watch the games. By mid-May the season is over and Kobs Field has a beautiful look to it—and no team to play on it. Ridiculous! There is no varsity sport for students to watch during the summer and baseball would be a perfect fit.

On other issues:

To me, Title Nine is not the answer for college athletic

departments. I believe revenue sports should be separated from non-revenue sports. It should not be a male-female issue. College sports can only exist in most athletic departments today if funds can be raised from the public. The public doesn't care about Title Nine—the public buys tickets via the law of supply and demand.

I do not support the theory that football needs unlimited resources, either. Why do schools need all those players on scholarship? Only 11 go on the field at one time. If every school operates under the same rules, it will not affect competitive balance. As George Perles suggests, I would eliminate spring football and let all players, including the incoming freshmen, have one more week in August to practice. Players can then spend the spring either concentrating on their academics or working part-time jobs, or both. I do not believe the quality of the game will suffer with fewer players or fewer practices.

Agents are another issue in which I have changed my mind over the years. I say if you can't beat them, join them. I'd consider allowing agents to have one week during the calendar year when they can sign up college players. It wouldn't matter if the player is a freshman or a senior. This way, college players would have some income to spend—their agents can give it to them. You could have some guidelines to make the agents conform to specified codes, but I don't see why it is in a college's best interest to constantly try to fight them. It is a battle colleges cannot win. Any other student on a campus can hire an agent for whatever purpose is desired—why not athletes? If agents paid players legally, it might keep many of them from turning professional early.

Do you know how many of the suggestions in this chapter will come to fruition? Probably very few. The hockey luxury boxes and the grass football field have a shot—beyond that I have my doubts. As Duffy Daugherty used to say, "It all makes so much sense, it will probably never happen."

CHAPTER 6

Go Blue

When your home base is Lansing and you cover two Big Ten schools, inevitably there becomes a problem over partiality toward one or the other. Clearly, Michigan State is the school of dominance in Lansing, but I have found a tremendous Michigan penetration, not only in this area, but around the state as well.

Many viewers did not attend either school. I have found that whichever has a hot team tends to widen its bandwagon with new fans. No wonder there are so many Michigan football fans around the state. They want to root for someone and it might as well be a winner—a big winner at that.

The Michigan-Michigan State relationship is a spirited rivalry, as most of you know. It is probably bigger between the fans than it is amongst the teams and coaches. Athletes and coaches from each school tend to be friendly with each other and have a mutual respect. Of course each wants to win when the two schools meet, but the ferocity isn't always the same as some fans treat it.

Gus Ganakas and Johnny Orr were close friends except when their teams met on the basketball court during the 1970s. They recruited against each other and their jobs depended, in some measure, on beating each other. But they were genuine, good guys and they liked being in each other's company in the off-season.

One summer Orr invited Gus and me to play golf with him in Ann Arbor. Johnny is an avid golfer and he had access to many courses. He hosted us at Radrick Farms with his friend Jim Caras, who went on to become Michigan's golf coach.

We bet a few bucks in this foursome and we had a great time.

Orr is one of two people in the world who can crack me up at a moment's notice. Baseball pitcher Dick Radatz is the other. We all play with about the same ability and while we laughed hard for four hours, we also had a spirited match. Afterward, Orr invited us to his home for dinner. During that evening, Gus and John traded coaching horror stories and the subject of Bobby Knight came up. Knight was very friendly with both Orr and Gus.

"I really envy Knight," Orr told us. "He treats those b———— - the way I wish I could."

Gus and I still have not forgotten that evening, nor that line. John loved Michigan and he had good success as the basketball coach. But he was never happy with the salary Don Canham paid him so he left for Iowa State, almost strictly because he was offered a larger salary. Football would always be king at Michigan. At Iowa State, football was a perennial loser and John had a chance to be a big star. For the most part, his teams were pretty good and the Cyclones fans loved his humor and his personality.

Another time, my brother hosted the three of us for golf at Birmingham Country Club near Detroit, where he was the manager. We had to play with a member of the club and the guy just happened to be a Michigan alum. As we waited on the first tee after our introduction, I wondered out loud, "Where are all the Michigan State guys on these courses?"

Orr had a ready answer. "They're all downtown playing at Palmer Park."

Don Canham was the best athletic director I ever met. He is a good friend and had a vision far beyond his peers. He had a great set-up at Michigan, which helped him immensely. His relationship with the school's various presidents was solid until he stepped down. Canham's best move obviously was to hire Bo Schembechler as football coach. Together, Canham and Bo helped Michigan achieve an incredible level of success during Bo's 21-year tenure as head coach. Bo won 17 of 21 games against Michigan State. No wonder Michigan fans always tried to play down the significance of the rivalry with the Spartans.

Canham was a no-nonsense guy. He knew how to invest his department's money. He had great rapport with the national media, as well as with students writing for the school paper. He was innovative. He and Bo disagreed at times, but they had a rock solid respect for each other. They had the relationship that others around the country should try to emulate. They needed each other to succeed and both knew it. Other schools around the country would always call Canham for his advice and counsel.

One day I went to interview Canham. While I was waiting in his outer office, his secretary picked up the phone to call in a new investment for the school's athletic department. "Mr. Canham would like $450,000 used to purchase more GM stock," she said. He moved the school's money all around to get the maximum bang for the buck.

Once in his office, Don was on the phone and motioned me to sit down.

"I don't care if they like it or not. If they want to cheerlead at the next game they will not do any more back flips. I'm not taking the liability for an accident." I don't know who he was talking to, but he slammed down the phone.

"Our cheerleaders want to do those dangerous back flips at all these games and they think they have the right to pick out the routine," he told me. "It doesn't work that way. I'm not going to be responsible when one of them gets paralyzed." That ended the back flips.

It comes as no surprise to me that since Canham left Michigan, the school has struggled far beyond the problems he ever encountered. Canham's book, published last year, criticizes the changes in Michigan's current athletic system. He was very critical of University of Michigan President James Duderstadt, who decided to become more involved with athletic department policy.

Since Canham's departure, Michigan has gone through four athletic directors, Tom Goss being the current office holder. Coaches have been fired, NCAA investigations have occurred and some athletes have struggled with the law. Canham never seemed to have as many difficulties in his total tenure as Michigan has experienced in the years since he left.

Another one of my favorite people is Schembechler. He has treated me well over the years and he has given me some excellent career advice. Despite his fiery personality during his coaching days, I never had a problem with him.

One day I visited Bo for a springtime interview. As I waited in his outer office, I heard screaming among Bo and his assistant coaches behind closed doors. They were watching film of a spring practice session and arguing over who was playing well and who was not. This went on for about 15 minutes and it got loud and sometimes nasty. I wondered what I was getting myself into that day when abruptly the door opened and out walked Bo.

"Hi Tim, great to see you. Come on in." His smile was wide and his demeanor cordial.

"I hope I didn't interrupt anything," I told him.

"Oh, we have some minor disagreements every now and then—nothing major."

I loved Bo's intensity as a coach. No one could intimidate him. He fully expected success and would never accept failure.

Duffy fooled him the first year Bo became head coach and Bo never forgot it. The 1969 UM-MSU game was played in East Lansing and Duffy's team was a distinct underdog. The Spartans installed a brand new veer offense the week of the game which featured the running of quarterback Bill Triplett, a player of average ability. The Spartans had been annihilated the previous two weeks by Notre Dame and Ohio State, and for all the world this looked like another lop-sided loss. Not that day. The Spartans had the Wolverines off-balance all game and won 23-12. They didn't fool many other teams en route to a 4-6 season record while Michigan went on to play in the Rose Bowl.

I have long felt two things about Bo. First, many Michigan people never appreciated him because he struggled in bowl games. But because of his personality and his great teams, Michigan Stadium was filled with more than 100,000 fans every Saturday and those fans rarely went home having just watched a loss. Winning can spoil fans and Bo clearly spoiled many of the faithful. Some of them felt his time had come once he announced his retirement and I couldn't believe that any Michigan fan could be happy to see him move on.

Secondly, Bo never had a chance with the Detroit Tigers. Had Tom Monaghan let him run the team in his own way, I absolutely believe that franchise would have been much more competitive. Bo struggled to adapt to pro sports, but what did him in was the Tigers' tight budget. He was handcuffed in making personnel moves and once he figured out he had little chance to succeed on his own merits, he knew it was time to part ways. Bo had some solid ideas to help the Tigers advance past many of their outmoded ways, but budget constraints always did him in.

I was fortunate enough to do the play by play of a number of the Fab Five's basketball games on television during their two years together. Those players knew they had star power from the beginning. They always treated me well whenever I spoke with them, but they were a handful for coach Steve Fisher.

During their freshman season, I worked Michigan's game at Wisconsin, where the Badgers were an average team. I attended the morning shoot-around and was amazed at what I witnessed. While the coaches were going through pre-game instructions, Jalen Rose, Chris Webber and several others were paying absolutely no attention at mid-court. They didn't listen to a word that was being said and I was surprised that Fisher didn't seem to notice. Michigan lost that night, 98-80.

The Fab Five were famous wherever they went. When they'd take the floor in opposing arenas, they were booed mercilessly. It was a testimony to their talent and the fact that they were from Michigan. I never had problems with Fisher, but he would never open up with me. I always felt he was hesitant to talk openly with me for some reason. He was always polite, but rarely gave me anything of substance.

Michigan's tradition will forever be difficult for Michigan State to overcome. There will always be moments when a Spartan team will beat the Wolverines. But Michigan has good location, plenty of available resources, and a national name to help it above and beyond most other Big Ten schools.

I've always wondered about the popularity of basketball at Michigan, however. I have never worked or attended a game in Crisler Arena that there weren't numerous empty seats. The tickets may all have been sold, but I can't ever recall a "jam-packed house." Michigan is first and foremost a football school and likely always will be.

When Gary Moeller was axed as head coach I thought there was a narrow window of opportunity for Michigan State to make up some ground in the rivalry. Clearly the program was in disarray and the timing was such that no national search could be made to find a big name successor. Lloyd Carr almost assuredly would never have landed the job in any other circumstances. No one knew what to expect when he was named head coach.

I felt Michigan might struggle for awhile. If you call four-loss seasons a struggle, then Michigan struggled. I thought there might be enough uncertainty in Carr's future that Michigan State could close the recruiting gap. And while the Spartans have recruited well under Nick Saban, for the most part, Michigan is now recruiting off a national championship.

And no one ever mentions Lloyd Carr's name as someone who will soon head off to the NFL.

I admire Carr, but not because of the 1997 season. The previous December, I introduced him at a Detroit News high school all-star banquet in Dearborn. I had never met him before. His team had just upset Ohio State to save its season, so he was in a pretty good mood. He was very easy-going and cordial with everyone and he mixed easily with the high school players and their parents.

His speech was not full of laughs, but it was inspirational and from the heart. I thought he was very genuine. I like the fact that he does not seem to overreact to problems during a season. He doesn't seem to get too high or too low after games. If he can maintain his demeanor and his personality he could have many more hugely successful seasons to come. He got some good advice a year ago from Schembechler.

Carr was struggling under the pressure of winning. He went to Bo for advice and Schembechler told him to pay no attention to outside fans and media but rather just concentrate on doing the best job he could. Carr heeded Bo's counsel and Michigan ended up 12-0. The ghost of Schembechler continues to haunt the Big Ten!

Through the years I have been accused of being anti-Michigan, pro-Michigan, a Michigan State homer, a traitor (to both schools), etc. I do not openly root for either one of them for the sake of simply being professional. I have some coaching friends I privately root for and spend time with socially, but when I anchor TV or talk on the radio I am merely passing on information about the two schools' teams that I think people would be interested in hearing about.

I understand that much of my audience is Michigan State fans, so I tend to cater to that group's interests much of the time. But I am absolutely not for nor against Michigan, nor any other school or professional team. If you think I am, I will not argue with you. I am honestly sharing with you how I personally feel and I'll let it go at that.

Joe Falls has struggled for years with a number of readers who have always accused him of being anti-Michigan State. My telling them that he is not never changes their opinions. I used to argue with them—but not any more. It's not worth the time and effort. People are going to think what they are going to think.

The fact that Michigan State was involved in more controversies than Michigan over the past 30 years is the key reason for this attitude in my judgment. Joe commented on controversial stories and most of them involved Michigan State. Hence, some decided he was anti-MSU. Joe was smart enough to decide many years ago not to worry about what people thought.

Michigan does have one thing going for it in football that I think Michigan State should adopt—uniform uniformity! Michigan's football uniforms basically never change. The helmets are known all over the country and the uniforms are always maize and blue with block 'M's pretty much in the same location. The traditional schools never change their football uniforms—Penn State, Notre Dame, Alabama, and Southern Cal to name a few.

Michigan State has colors that few major schools have—green and white. If it was my call, I'd make the uniforms the same each season. They should look like the MSU uniforms of the 1950s when the teams were great. Green helmets with one white stripe down the middle and numbers on each side (just like Alabama, only green). They should have white pants with one green stripe. The home jerseys should be green with plain white numerals and perhaps several white stripes on the sleeves—nothing more! Then this look should remain the same every year so people always associate it with Michigan State.

Every year, the MSU teams take the field with newly designed uniforms. I say traditional teams should continue to wear traditional uniforms. It's the schools begging for a new identity who always change. Indiana even wore black jerseys during the 1997 season, for crying out loud! No offense Spartans, but your current uniforms look like they were designed by a contemporary MSU art student who received a failing grade. Now does that opinion make me anti-MSU and pro-Michigan? I'm sure some readers out there will think so despite my best protests. Right, Joe?

CHAPTER 7

Big Ten

You know the sports world is crazy when a college conference calls itself the Big Ten and in reality there are 11 schools in the league. Go figure.

Because television has become so dominant in the fabric of Division I college sports, the nation's 110 or so football schools have had to consolidate the leagues so as to get a better revenue deal. Hence the Southwest Conference is long gone and the Southeastern Conference consists of some schools that in reality are not located in the southeast. Now we have the Big 12 and the Big Ten plus Penn State. What happens when the Big Ten finally adds a twelfth school is open to anyone's speculation.

All of my life I have been a Big Ten guy. When my family moved to East Lansing in 1955 from Massachusetts, I immediately learned that Michigan State was a relatively new member of the conference. I could almost immediately recite the ten league schools in alphabetical order which would come in handy throughout my professional life.

Like all other conferences, the Big Ten brags that it is the best, the most highly respected and has the most fans.

Here's my take: When integration began to fully involve all of the major football schools, the Big Ten no longer attracted as many quality minority athletes as it did in the 1950s and 1960s. The sunbelt schools suddenly realized that quality minority athletes were right in their backyard and now schools like Miami of Florida, Florida State, Auburn, Arizona and Arizona State, just to name a few, gradually became competitive with everyone.

Even Notre Dame's spectacular 1966 national championship

team had all of one black athlete—Alan Page. That was the team that played Michigan State to the famous 10-10 tie in East Lansing. Imagine—one black athlete on a team of any prominence at a national school like Notre Dame and that was a scant 32 years ago.

Today Big Ten football teams struggle to grab recruits just like everyone else. The traditional schools will probably always fare well—Michigan, Ohio State and Penn State. The rest will have varying degrees of success depending, in large measure, on who the head coach is. When Penn State was added to the league, my first reaction was that many Big Ten football teams that are already struggling just got another loss pinned on their record.

The Big Ten does have some solid claims that are hard to dispute. Its schools are all educationally tradition-rich with large football stadiums filled with many fans. Big Ten attendance probably will always be tops in the nation or very close.

Because the conference is located in the middle of a large population base it will always draw heavy television coverage. All the networks want to carry Big Ten football and basketball if possible.

Michigan's 1997 co-national football championship is probably a fluke. Most coaches will readily admit that it is too difficult for a Big Ten team to run its schedule undefeated and the addition of Penn State made it all the more complicated. Still, Penn State and Michigan have each fashioned a perfect season in the last five years.

I have covered basketball and football games at all of the schools many times. I have my favorites and favorite memories that have built up over the years.

The conference office has moved around suburban Chicago several times and I have known two of the commissioners.

Wayne Duke is retired now. He was hired in 1971 when Duffy Daugherty was still the football coach at Michigan State and Duffy heavily endorsed him when I interviewed him about it.

Wayne had his detractors in the league over the years—it must go with the territory. But he survived to retire and I still see him occasionally at various games from time to time.

Jim Delany is a no-nonsense guy who cannot be intimidated. I like him for that reason alone. He is a shrewd television negotiator and he has a contemporary way of thinking about college athletics. He is a former North Carolina basketball player and some of the football coaches believe he is too basketball-oriented. Delany helped move the league to a Big Ten post-season basketball tournament.

Bo Schembechler is not one of his fans. Delany alerted the officials to penalize Bo when he stepped away from the coaches' boxes on the sidelines at football games. And Bo was miffed when the Big Ten athletic directors were not consulted about Penn State's admission to the conference. That move alone caused Bo to decide to get out of his athletic director job at Michigan.

There is no sense reminiscing about visits to Michigan State and Michigan, right? Too close by. But here are thoughts and memories about the other big nine schools in the Big Ten Conference:

ILLINOIS. This school is always in first place in the league alphabetically. Athletically it has been a struggle. Illinois has been the victim in football of hiring the wrong coaches over and over again. Gary Moeller was fired as the football coach there, but in the same job at Michigan he had a 44-13 record. I guess it's easier to get players to go to Michigan than Illinois. And the last time I looked, Illinois just put together a nice 0-11 record. How can the state school, just two hours south of Chicago, struggle to find athletes?

MSU fans can easily drive to games at Illinois in five hours or less. It's all interstate highway and I regularly drive there in the winter when I am assigned basketball games.

I had an MSU basketball telecast at Illinois the night the Persian Gulf War broke out. When we went on the air, we didn't know if any stations along the network were carrying our broadcast. We thought they'd all be carrying news reports of the war. Most did carry the game and the Spartans won behind a great performance from Steve Smith.

The Illinois basketball arena is a round dome which was built in 1963 for $8 million. It is still in beautiful shape today and it seats 16,000 fans. When the Illini beat Michigan State 84-63 last February, it was the most noise I had ever heard from a crowd anywhere for any game I had ever worked. You would have thought the Illini had won the NCAA championship that night.

The campus is rich with traditional architecture and it is smack dab in the middle of town. There will never be a downhill ski team at Illinois. The land is flat for miles around. And there's plenty of parking available between the football and basketball arenas because they are across the street from each other. There is also a large cemetery behind the east football stands. How symbolic since many Illinois football dreams have been buried after another disappointing home loss.

INDIANA. My birthplace. My dad was a young faculty member at the Indiana University School of Business for a couple of years and he still has friends in Bloomington. We lived in the old Hoosier Courts, a quonset hut community, which long since has been razed. When I'd tell Bobby Knight where we lived, he always gave me a curious eye because he'd never heard of "Hoosier Courts." Like I say Bob, they tore down the place.

Bloomington is easy to get to by car, some four and a half hours from Lansing. In 1964, our entire family of five went to Bloomington for the Michigan State vs. Indiana game during a gorgeous fall weekend. Natch, the Spartans made enough mistakes to lose 27-20 and this was the year before their great Rose Bowl team of 1965.

Indiana had just built its new football stadium several years earlier. It seats 52,000 and has the best sight lines of any stadium in the Big Ten. One reason is because there are usually only about 35,000 fans in the place.

In 1995, George Perles and I broadcast the Michigan State at Indiana football game on one of the most miserable weather days I can ever remember. This was in November, the week after the Spartans had upset Michigan in East Lansing in Nick Saban's first year.

I took my entire family and bought four $20 tickets the week of the game. Nice move. Because of the weather there couldn't have been 5,000 people in the stands. The ushers were letting people in for free. Indiana ran off 22 plays to the Spartans, three in the first quarter and still trailed 21-0. The Hoosiers' special teams weren't too special that day—they gave up three long touchdowns on kick returns.

Attending an Indiana basketball game is a special experience and I have been there many times. As you know, Bob Knight is the king in Bloomington. The basketball arena is not fitting for a program like Indiana's, nor for a coach with the presence that Knight commands.

In January, 1996, Knight took me on a tour of the place the day of a game against the Spartans. He calls the Assembly Hall "a monstrosity" because there are so many bad seats that are so high and so far away from the floor. As Knight says, the basketball arena was designed by the same guy who drew up the football stadium and therefore they look somewhat the same.

There is a tremendous souvenir shop underneath the stands at Assembly Hall. I always browse through it before games to check out any new items. After Knight's tour in 1996, I noticed in the shop that Bob Knight dolls, standing four feet tall, were for sale. If the price tag was around $100, I would have bought one and given it to my brother as a Christmas present. He attended Indiana.

The elderly shop lady informed me that the price was $800, thank you.

"I'll bet you don't sell any of these," I dead panned.

"Excuse me sir," she answered immediately. "The doll maker signed and made 800 and we have about 150 left. They went on sale a month ago. We will soon be sold out."

I stood corrected.

The population base around Bloomington is limited and it hurts football attendance greatly. Many of the basketball fans come from Indianapolis, 50 miles to the north. They arrive early and many are elderly. They are all dressed in solid red and white and many of the men wear coats and ties. The students are perfectly well-behaved in the Bob Knight tradition. Most of them are dressed far better than what you see from students in other arenas.

As for Knight, he never arrives on the floor until just prior to the opening tip, which is also his pattern for road games. Or as Gus Ganakas always says, "He doesn't arrive until the bitter end."

As you know, Knight is revered in Bloomington, but he always speaks very highly of the school and its President. Knight has always been close with the various Indiana presidents over the years in stark contrast to coaches I have known at other schools.

He does many things on campus for non-basketball students that don't receive much publicity. What is also ironic is that one of his best friends for years was a sportswriter—Bob Hammel. Bob was the sports editor of the Bloomington newspaper until he retired several years ago. He made all the road trips with the Indiana team.

Whenever Bob Knight leaves Indiana it will be like Woody Hayes leaving Ohio State. Both will have had their detractors at the end, but both will be sorely missed from the standpoint that they commanded such a presence during their careers.

IOWA. The Hawkeyes are the biggest deal in this state because there are no major league teams. The campus dominates Iowa City and I claim it is more difficult to get to Iowa City than it is to Penn State. The Cedar Rapids airport is 17 miles to the north—at least State College, Pennsylvania has an airport only five minutes from campus.

Iowa fans follow their teams all over the place and they have grown accustomed to the down home corn pone humor of long-time football coach Hayden Fry. His teams have usually been competitive, but Iowa football likely will never crack the big three of Michigan, Ohio State and Penn State on a regular basis.

I think Carver-Hawkeye Arena is the best basketball facility in the Big Ten for several reasons. There is no balcony. There are 44 rows in a bowl-shaped configuration, much like Michigan's football stadium. This prevents spectators from feeling like they are in a first class or second class status. The top row is at ground level with a wide concourse all the way around the building. The downside is parking— there just isn't much around the place because it is built inside a hill.

With a fanatical following it is always tough for visiting teams to win in Iowa City in either football or basketball. The basketball crowd was almost eerily silent in the 1997-98 season game when Michigan State pulled away to a 78-57 win, one of the worst home losses an Iowa basketball team had ever suffered.   MINNESOTA. Located on the Mississippi River, this campus is much different looking from the others in the conference. It is part of an urban setting and the old Memorial Stadium, home of the Gopher football teams, is now long gone. The school now uses the Metrodome, which is about four miles away, downtown. I believe the lack of an on-campus stadium has hurt Minnesota's growth in this sport. It has been down for years since the great Bobby Bell teams of the early 1960s.

Minnesota has a gorgeous new hockey arena, named after former long-time coach John Mariucci. Almost all of the hockey games are televised and so are the state tournament high school games. It is a hockey state with no NHL team anymore, at least at the moment.

Old Williams Arena has been renovated and like Jenison Fieldhouse at MSU, the seating capacity was reduced during the refurbishment. It now seats 14,000 and the views are all good. One reason is because the floor is raised and that drives visiting coaches nut.

Jud Heathcote never missed an opportunity to rip Minnesota for having a raised basketball floor and, half in jest, he has always hoped some player would get severely injured falling off it. He could then sue the school for millions and get rid of the floor once and for all.

Indeed it does look strange for coaches to sit on stools in front of their benches during the games. When I broadcast there, you look up at the action since press row is beneath the floor. The place can get very loud at times. When I worked the Michigan State game at Minneapolis in March, 1997, when the Gophers celebrated their Big Ten title, I didn't think the proceedings would ever end. They took place immediately after the game and none of the fans left for at least half an hour. It helps such celebrations when the home team wins the game and Minnesota rallied to beat Michigan State that night, 81-74.

Who will ever forget the press facilities in the old football stadium. There was a high school-like edifice on each side of the field—one for broadcasters and one for the writers. There were no such things as luxury boxes in those days. The lighting and plumbing were incredibly primitive and for such a prominent school, the place was an embarrassment. Parking was scant and the weather was always cold and—well no wonder Minnesota has had trouble recruiting good football players over the years.

Minnesota fans can drive to very few events. The hardy ones can drive to Iowa, Wisconsin and Northwestern, but the rest of the trips almost always must be made by air.

NORTHWESTERN. This school's recruiting problems over the years have centered around one problem—academic admission. It's tough to get into Northwestern and if the good athletes from the Chicago area don't have sufficient grades in high school, they can always go somewhere else. I say this and then I wonder why schools like Stanford always do so well in so many sports with tough admission standards also.

Northwestern has been an underachiever in my book. It has a

fabulous academic reputation and its campus is gorgeous, situated on the shore of Lake Michigan. The glitter of Chicago is nearby. It has easy access to many recruiting areas. Yet until Gary Barnett came on board, Northwestern was a complete joke in football.

It's the one trip visiting fans always like to make. Plenty of tickets are usually available and a weekend in Chicago can be great. The visiting team usually wins also.

I thought Barnett's Rose Bowl season was one of the all-time miracles in modern-day college sports. How he took that rag tag operation and won as many games as he did will forever be a mystery to me. He beat Michigan in Ann Arbor and he beat Penn State in Evanston. He did not have to play Ohio State nor Michigan State in that glory year of 1995 and that helped also.

Since then, Northwestern has dramatically upgraded its stadium and the lousy press box is now gone. The school has now gone the luxury box route. It has also added an indoor football facility which is smaller than others, but still efficient. It has also added a new football office.

The old dirt floor of McGaw Hall is long gone for the basketball team. It is now Welsh-Ryan Arena inside of McGaw Hall. It seats 8,000 and is very comfortable, but I doubt Northwestern will ever challenge for Big Ten basketball supremacy. It just does not have enough tradition or low enough entrance standards.

I watched the 1966 MSU football team win in Evanston, 22-0, en route to its unbeaten season. Bubba Smith had a big performance that day. But I've seen other MSU teams stink the place out by failing to get motivated. It's been easy to look past a Northwestern team over the years. Very few fans attended the games.

I remember one memorable basketball telecast at Northwestern back in the early 1980s. My station was televising the game, but there was no network coverage that night. The officials got confused and failed to call TV timeouts since they thought there was no broadcast whatsoever.

The Spartans were struggling and Jud was dying for a timeout. He sent his assistant coach, Edgar Wilson, over to our table, to ask when we were going to take one. Pretty soon the officials got in on it, including Phil Bova, who still works Big Ten games today.

Everyone was arguing over why the officials had no knowledge of television coverage that night. They all finally decided to blame me and I told them (right on the air) that it wasn't my responsibility to notify the officials that we were televising the game. State went on to lose that night, but I think Jud was more upset with his team than he was with the missed early TV time-out.

OHIO STATE. Woody Hayes. So much for Ohio State now let's move on to Penn State. Or so it would seem, right? When I think of Ohio State, I think of Woody Hayes and everything and everyone else comes in a distant second. We'll never see another like him. When you watched the Buckeyes what did your eyes watch the most, the sideline or the field?

I don't know about you, but the Ohio State-Michigan football game lost something for me when Woody left. Beating Woody's successor, Earle Bruce, just didn't seem to make the rivalry the same. They still miss him in Columbus.

One of the greatest Michigan State football victories of all time was achieved in Columbus on a rain-swept October day in 1966. The Spartans had embarrassed Hayes the year before in East Lansing, with a 32-7 win. Ohio State's vaunted three yards and a cloud of dust ground game was held to -51 yards for the day. Woody would make Duffy pay the next year in Columbus.

For some reason I wore a suit to the game and got absolutely drenched. The Spartans trailed 8-3 when they went on an 80-yard touchdown drive late in the game. They faked a kick on the point after touchdown and the two points were crucial.

Woody was not about to kick for a tie with a field goal in the final seconds. There was no overtime then and only victory would do—not a tie. The Buckeyes could not score and the Spartans escaped, 11-8. They won a second straight Big Ten title with a perfect conference record.

This is another painless, four-hour car ride from Lansing if you've ever thought about attending a game in Columbus. And wait until you see the new $105 million basketball/hockey arena which is about to open. The school says no other arena in the country will be as nice. Now the Buckeyes just need some decent basketball teams to fill the place.

No football coach ever has security in Columbus. John Cooper has survived despite winning just one time in nine years over Michigan. The rest of his record is spectacular, but he is still not very well liked by many of the Buckeye faithful.

I broadcast the Rice-Ohio State football game for the Big Ten network on opening day, September, 1996. What a scene. On a perfect day, I arrived at the stadium at 9:30 a.m., figuring I'd beat all the traffic and have an easy time parking and getting set up.

After crossing the Olentangy River on Lane Avenue, the place was mobbed by thousands of scarlet and gray-clad Buckeye fans who had assembled for breakfast and weren't leaving until well after the game. The Ohio State band had already arrived and was warming up for its pregame and halftime shows. This wasn't even a big game. Rice eventually would lose 70-7 and it could have been a lot worse. But there are only about six days a year for an Ohio State football game in Columbus and the locals there make a full day of it. They have Woody to thank for it. The souvenir shops around the stadium still have plenty of Woody Hayes memorabilia.

PENN STATE. It's a beautiful place located at least seven and a half hours by car from mid-Michigan. Penn State looks like a Big Ten school. The campus dominates the small town and it has the old-time traditional college look, nestled amongst the mountains.

They keep saying they are going to expand the runway so bigger planes can land but until then, it's an airline adventure. There is a commuter non-stop to and from Detroit now. Some football teams fly two small planes, like George Perles did. Or they take the one big plane and land in Harrisburg. It's a two-and-a-half hour bus ride from there.

The football stadium has been expanded several times and it looks like a giant erector set. It is located in the middle of farm land, so there is plenty of parking.

The new Bryce Jordan Center is probably the worst of the new arenas I have ever seen. The seats are too far back from the floor and the "end zone" seats seem like miles away. I do not know how they'll ever fill the place. Even their former basketball coach, Bruce Parkhill, admits the school made a mistake and should have used a design closer to Michigan State's Breslin Center. Wrong. A duplicate of Iowa's Carver-Hawkeye arena would have been the way to go.

Joe Paterno owns the place. He is revered there and he doesn't add all the baggage of a prima donna either. Paterno sure looks good for a guy past 70. He recently donated several million dollars to the school's library fund because he said the money had accumulated and he didn't know what else to do with it.

When Penn State first joined the Big Ten, Paterno toured all of the other conference schools. When he visited in Lansing, a big reception was held for him and I was invited. I spent several minutes with him alone and then interviewed him on camera.

Several days later I was stunned to receive a full-page letter from Paterno thanking me for my time with him. I couldn't believe he had taken the time to write and I am sure he wrote to others in my business too. He wanted to make a good first impression among the Big Ten veterans and he sure won me over.

I like the way Penn State's football team looks. It maintains its tradition. Simple uniforms that never change and no players' names on the back. Penn State is Penn State and players feel honored to wear the uniform. It is bigger than their own last name. Indiana basketball players also do not wear their names on their uniforms. Paterno and Knight. Principled guys who build off the tradition of their sport at their school. Both huge winners too.

I worked the 1996 Penn State football game at Giants Stadium against Temple. Only 24,000 fans showed up—it was considered a Temple home game.

When Paterno ran on the field all the fans went crazy—he was the big star. Penn State won 41-0 and it could have been worse except that Joe had pity for his peer on the other side of the field, Ron Dickerson, his former assistant coach.

Penn State has clearly added quality to the Big Ten. I claim the schools that have trouble beating Michigan and Ohio State now have another mountain to climb in Happy Valley. When Paterno leaves, Fran Ganter, his longtime assistant, will likely take over and the winning will continue. Ganter was the guy who could have had the Michigan State job after George Perles was fired, but his indecision turned the tide to Nick Saban. Ganter might have struggled in East Lansing because recruiters would have always claimed he'd go home to Penn State as soon as Paterno stepped aside.

PURDUE. The greatest individual effort in a Michigan State football game I ever saw occurred during a battle I worked on radio at Purdue in October 1971. George Blaha and I called the Spartans' 43-10 victory on a day when Eric "the Flea" Allen ran for 350 yards, then an NCAA record. Duffy put Allen back in the game just long enough to reach his milestone, then took him out for good. He could have run for more than 400 the way things were going. Allen had broken four sensational runs for touchdowns during the day which left the crowd awe struck.

Purdue doesn't need a new football coach, it needs a new interstate highway to Lansing. You drive south of Fort Wayne on I-69, then the hassles begin. It is 108 miles of tough driving to get there after leaving the interstate and the trip is always a bit more than four hours start to finish.

Ross-Ade Stadium is a great place to watch a game. The Purdue band is probably the best in the Big Ten, at least the one with the most tradition. The "golden girl" and the "silver twins" are a big deal to the Boilermakers and they claim they have the biggest drum in the world. It truly is big, I'll give them that.

Some Purdue fans have a basketball inferiority complex to Indiana, like Michigan State fans have to Michigan in football. In reality, Purdue's all-time basketball record is as good or better than Indiana's. Mackey Arena was built bargain basement and it has a terrific atmosphere. It is a much better facility than Indiana's Assembly Hall. Gene Keady has made life generally miserable for Bobby Knight over the years—the Hoosiers clearly do not dominate Purdue in basketball.

Keady is not the prima donna off the court that he is on it. Most of his act during games is just for effect, both with the crowd and the officials. He is approachable and he has a sense of humor.

Whether Purdue ever competes for a Big Ten football title again remains to be seen. The Boilermakers went 9-3 during the 1997 season, but got some tremendous breaks along the way. Michigan State absolutely handed them a victory that probably cost the Spartans a berth in a Florida bowl game.

Under long time coach Jack Mollenkopf in the 1960s, Purdue was pretty good. Bob Griese played a great game at quarterback in Spartan Stadium in 1966. That was when the Spartans were loaded, and they beat the Boilers 41-20 that day. Because of the no repeat rule, Michigan State did not make it to the Rose Bowl after that season, Purdue did.

WISCONSIN. The home of Bucky Badger. Wisconsin was awful in football for years and then Barry Alvarez came along and now the Badgers are a bit better than average. Alvarez got a ten-year contract, much in the way George Perles got one at Michigan State. He had one Rose Bowl season and the school panicked that he might leave. Now they can't get rid of him for awhile and Wisconsin has basically said without Alvarez no one else can come in and win.

The school finally eliminated that ancient basketball arena that made Jenison Fieldhouse look like a palace. It was cramped and cold and dirty and it had no parking. Add the fact that the Wisconsin teams were rarely any good and you see why the sport has struggled. Coach Dick Bennett better find a way to win and entertain the fans more than scoring 40 points a game or he'll be long gone—that new Kohl Center has 16,000 seats to fill and plenty of luxury boxes too.

Madison must be gorgeous in the summer time, located on two beautiful lakes. One of them is Lake Mendota. When Jud Heathcote coached his last MSU game there he was interviewed for that day's pregame newspaper story.

"I won't miss this place," he was quoted as saying. "It's always cold when we come here and there's always snow covering Lake Menadini or whatever they call it."

NOTRE DAME. What a school to round out the Big Ten to twelve right? It likely will happen. The Big Ten will only take schools in all sports and Notre Dame must give up its football independence.

Ohio State's John Cooper thinks the Big Ten should boycott Notre Dame until it joins the league. Schools like Michigan State need Notre Dame every other year to play at home in order to sell season football tickets.

My dad took my brother and me to the 1965 game in South Bend in which that great Spartan team won, 12-3. I met my wife at the 1983 game in South Bend and in 1967 I broadcast the first basketball game on radio at the new Convocation Center. Lew Alcindor (now Kareem Abdul Jabbar) and his UCLA Bruins played in that opener.

In 1973, I decided to take a date to the Michigan State at Notre Dame basketball game. I would pick her up in Birmingham, then turn around and drive to South Bend. When you're dating you'll go to almost any lengths to have a good time.

Just past Brighton I ran into heavy fog. My brand new Camaro convertible ran into a chain reaction pile up and I was for-

tunate to escape serious injury. The car was destroyed and I barely got out of the mess before it got hit by an oncoming semi truck.
The police called my mother who saw the car before she saw me
several hours later. Shaken up as she was it could have been much
worse. I never made it to South Bend that day. I also never had a
chance to take that girl out on another date.

Going to a football game in South Bend is an experience like
a basketball game at Indiana. Each is unique from other schools.
They are richly traditional. They are worth enjoying. They are
what make college sports something special over whatever you
might find from the pros.

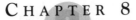

CHAPTER 8

Predictions

During the 1973 football season, I wrote for the Football News, published weekly in Detroit. I had met the publisher, the late Roger Stanton, and we became friends. He asked me to write for his paper and predict college games along with several others each week during the season. Predicting the outcome of games in any sport is fun for fans and is a big part of media coverage: Point spreads are published in newspapers and predictions are regular features in many publications. Office pools are common.

Growing up I always thought I was pretty good at picking games, especially football. In 1973, I was also calling Michigan State football games on radio. The final week of the season I called the Spartans' game at Iowa. This was in Denny Stolz' first year as head coach. The same day, Ohio State was playing at Michigan and as usual the Rose Bowl bid was on the line.

For whatever reason, I felt all week that the Wolverines and Buckeyes were so closely matched and played so conservatively that they would play a low scoring tie game. So in the Football News that week, Roger Stanton allowed me to insert the word "tie" next to my call for the Ohio State-Michigan game.

I took my dad to the Iowa game with me and the moment it was announced to the crowd that the game in Ann Arbor had ended 10-10 I couldn't wait for a commercial break to whip out the Football News to show everyone in our broadcast booth how smart I was.

Afterward I was interviewed about hitting that game on the nose, but it was not the zenith of my prediction career. That came in 1967 while I was still a student at Michigan State University.

At the time I was a freshman and dating a girl from my McDonel Hall dormitory whose family had just moved from Grosse Ile to southern California. As the Christmas holiday drew near she was trying to talk me into visiting her during the school break. One day at lunch she threw the school newspaper in front of me which advertised a college football prediction contest. It was sponsored by the Insurance Company of North America (INA). This was a national contest for college students with a grand prize of a trip for two to the Rose Bowl game. The prize included four nights in beautiful southern California with many extra activities during the trip.

Karen was insistent that I fill out the 30-game form and send it in. I completed it and gave it to her, not caring what she did with it.

The school break arrived and two days later I got a call from a representative of INA congratulating me on winning the national prediction contest—I was told I had picked the winners of all 30 games! I couldn't believe it and still didn't until the confirmation papers were delivered by courier to my parents' home in East Lansing the next day.

I took my brother with me on the trip and we enjoyed our Christmas holiday although I ended up spending more time with him than I did with Karen. Greg and I watched O. J. Simpson and the Southern Cal Trojans wear down Indiana, 14-3. We were treated like royalty all four days—staying at the Ambassador Hotel in Los Angeles. We attended a New Year's Eve party in the ballroom—the same ballroom where Presidential candidate Robert Kennedy would be shot to death less than six months later.

In my early television days I predicted Big Ten games on the air, but there was a problem every time I'd get to Michigan State. I got tired of being called a homer when I picked the Spartans to win and I also hated being called negative when I picked them to lose. My accuracy wasn't always top notch either—figuring that my talent had run out of gas I gave up predicting college football games formally years ago.

Once I was stopped by a police officer in East Lansing who thought I was traveling a bit faster than what the speed limit allowed. He recognized me and I was given an offer: "If you fill out my bowl prediction sheet in the staff pool, I will let you off with a warning."

No problem—I literally took his clipboard through the car window—and with his lights still flashing behind me, picked the winners of the upcoming bowl games for him. At your service, officer—always glad to help East Lansing's finest! I don't know how he ever made out because I don't remember who I picked for him, but I did go through all the theatrics of making it look like I was in deep thought while I was filling out his sheet.

Whether the colleges want to hear it or not, if gambling among fans was removed from sports, both pro and college, the interest level in these games from the general public would decline dramatically. College officials are all breathlessly talking about their concern about gambling on campuses these days, but I don't see it as big a problem as are some other issues. The point-shaving basketball scandals at Arizona State and Northwestern have brought this issue into a larger picture, but I see these more as isolated incidents than a forthcoming trend.

Point-shaving is too hard to pull off. Almost everyone who ever got involved was caught and few athletes are willing to take the risk for the pay-off. I just don't buy it as that big a problem. Are there student bookies on campuses? Of course. Is it worth getting hot and bothered about them? Well, alcohol seems to me to be a far bigger problem on campuses worth more scrutiny than a couple of student bookies trying to finance their way through school.

Betting on games is a matter of supply and demand. Almost all newspapers publish point spreads and injury reports. There is a demand for this information from readers. Almost all of them have writers predicting the outcome of games. Assuming that most people aren't compulsive gamblers, I believe office pools and small wagers between friends simply adds to fans' enjoyment of games. But no one should listen to my picks—the days of winning trips and correctly forecasting tie games are long gone!

CHAPTER 9

Magic

One Friday night in early December, 1974, the phone rang in the sports office at the old WJIM-TV studio. It was my friend, Fred Stabley, Jr., calling. He was a writer for the Lansing State Journal and he had just covered the Jackson Parkside at Lansing Everett High School basketball game.

"Have you seen this Everett sophomore, Earvin Johnson, yet?" he asked.

I had not. The season was young. Everett had just beaten Parkside 86-70 to move to 2-0 after an opening 44-43 win several days earlier against Holt.

"I want to give this guy a nickname," he went on, "and I want to see if you'll use it too. I want to nickname him 'Magic'. What do you think?"

"Too corny," I replied. "It'll never stick."

"Then give me some ideas," he went on.

"How about 'the franchise'," was the first thing that came to mind, lame as that sounded then and still sounds today.

"Well I'm going to use the nickname 'Magic" for Earvin Johnson in tomorrow's paper."

And perhaps the most familiar nickname in the entire world of sports was founded as simply as that.

The next morning I checked Fred's story and sure enough, there was the first use of the nickname "Magic." A star was born.

If you have lived anywhere around these parts, you may well know the rest of the story, as Paul Harvey would say it. And if you weren't around here from that December, 1974, period through the rest of the decade you missed the greatest sports era in mid-

Michigan history—bar none! Lucky me and lucky Fred. Not only were we around to witness it, we covered Earvin "Magic" Johnson from high school to his national championship days at Michigan State, to his departure for the NBA draft. And we'll never forget it.

A skinny black kid with a big afro haircut would soon become the rage of Michigan high school basketball from those early days of his sophomore season onward. And he wasn't all that happy to suit up in the red, white and blue of the Everett Vikings, at least in the beginning.

There was school bussing in Lansing in those days. He lived in the Sexton area and he planned on playing for the Big Reds with his friends, mostly black. Everett was mostly white. He had no option. He would have to enroll at a school where he knew very few of the students. He didn't know anything about the varsity coach, George Fox. He wanted to play for Doug Herner at Sexton, who in turn was counting on coaching this kid for a few years.

The rest is history. Earvin was one of two sophomores for the '74-'75 season on the Vikings' team. Larry Hunter, who averaged 9.9 points per game, was the other. Everett fashioned a 22-2 record and lost narrowly to Dearborn in the quarter-finals of the state tournament, 58-55.

I broadcast a number of those games on radio and before packed houses of 2,400 in the Vikings' gym. Everett started that season at 4-0 then lost 65-62 to Waverly. The Vikings rallied to win 18 straight before bowing out of the state tournament.

Earvin averaged 22 points and 17 rebounds per game as a tenth grader. He was the talk of high school basketball.

Everett had a 24-2 record during his junior year, losing at Christmas time to Detroit Northeastern, 63-58, and in the state semi-finals, 68-60 to Detroit Catholic Central. Earvin averaged 26 points per game and 17 rebounds the second time around. He was frustrated at putting together a 46-4 record over two seasons, but not playing yet in a state championship game. He would get one last shot.

The broadcast highlights of those first two seasons would come during the state tournament, especially at the Regionals in Kalamazoo. Western Michigan University's fieldhouse was the site and it was jammed with 9,800 fans whenever Everett appeared.

In Earvin's junior year, the Vikings would face Battle Creek Central in the championship game. My friend Jim Hornberger broadcast the games with me that season and we had to tape a pregame show. So he went down to interview Battle Creek's coach, Chuck Turner.

"How will you try to stop Earvin Johnson tonight?" Jim asked Turner. "Most teams zone him because he kills a man-to-man defense."

"We play man to man," Turner said. "That's our game. We don't change for just one player."

"Have you seen this guy play?" Jim asked a bit surprised.

"We've seen him. That's how we play defense."

"Good luck," Jim finished. "You're gonna need it."

Everett won 66-55 and Earvin dominated the game at both ends.

His senior year was an incredible spectacle. Michigan State was going through a 10-17 season under first-year coach Jud Heathcote, so the Spartans made little noise in town. Everett and Earvin Johnson were the big stories.

The recruiting battle, of course, was fierce and it boiled down to two schools—Michigan and Michigan State. Earvin was miffed that Gus Ganakas had been fired at MSU the year before. And Johnny Orr was working hard with his assistant Bill Frieder to land this magical player.

Everett cruised through the regular season. Earvin scored 54 points to break the city single-game record one night in a 103-52 win over Waverly. East Lansing lost a week later, 109-41.

Between those century mark games, Everett faced Eastern at MSU's Jenison Fieldhouse. They had met in the third game of the season with Everett winning 86-79. Jay Vincent was a solid player for Eastern and for this game, Jenison's 10,500 seats still would not be enough.

I sat high above the floor and broadcast the game on radio and watched Jay have his only moment of glory in high school against Earvin. The Quakers won 70-62 and they frustrated Earvin all night long. Paul Cook was Eastern's coach and he knew the Everett players about as well as George Fox did, so the Quakers were well prepared and ready.

By chance, the draw for the opening district game in the state tournament paired Everett and Eastern. What a shame they couldn't meet in the championship. Eastern hosted the district that season and the Don Johnson Fieldhouse would be packed with 4,400 fans.

I talked my boss, Hal Gross, into televising this game live. We had never done a live basketball telecast before. I had never broadcast a game on television before. Because Eastern was located less than a mile away from the WJIM Country House and had a high roof line, we discovered that we had the proper microwave equipment to get a television signal back to our studio. In those days we did not have "live trucks" like you see around the area today.

Everett dominated the game, winning 63-41 and the town was in a frenzy in the days leading up to the rubber match between the two schools. Earvin was sensational and I felt bad that Jay Vincent had never played on as much as a district champion in his high school career—all because Earvin played the exact same years at Everett.

The Vikings then blitzed East Lansing 70-33 and Sexton 81-45 to win the district title. Next up was unbeaten Howell in the Regional opener in Kalamazoo.

Howell must have had 5,000 fans in the fieldhouse that night. They felt they had a very good chance to spring an upset because they had scouted Everett for a long time and figured this match-up was coming. That final again—Everett 93, Howell 32, and it could have been much worse.

Everett whipped three more teams before meeting Birmingham Brother Rice in the state championship game at Crisler Arena in Ann Arbor. In those days, the semi-finals and finals were played one week apart. The media frenzy was unbelievable leading up to the game—Brother Rice was very good and led by coach Bill Norton, who would go on to become an assistant for a season to Jud Heathcote at Michigan State. Kevin Smith was Brother Rice's star player and would later sign on with the Spartans.

Smith hit a half court shot at the buzzer to send the game into overtime. There was no three-point shot then, otherwise Everett would have lost. Earvin dominated the game as never before, but he fouled out with a minute left in overtime and his team up by six points. The Vikings held on to win 62-56, shooting free throws in the final seconds to ice the victory.

It was truly a magical year—Earvin averaged 29 points per game and once again, 17 rebounds. He was all-world and he would travel overseas to play in a high school all-star game.

He had not tipped his hand on his college choice yet and that became a consuming story as the season wore on.

Of course, all the media wanted to land the big scoop—which school would get Magic Johnson? I long felt that Michigan was right in the hunt. Earvin questioned Jud Heathcote's vociferous ways with his players. He was impressed with Michigan's players when he visited the Wolverines' games in Ann Arbor. And he was still miffed that Gus Ganakas was no longer the Spartans' coach.

Jud retained Vernon Payne from Gus' staff as an assistant on his own and it would prove to be one of the wisest decisions he made in his entire career. Decision day was coming when Payne accepted the head coaching job at Wayne State.

Before leaving town, Vernon asked to visit with Earvin one last time. He convinced him that Michigan State was the place to go and Jud was the guy to play for because he would develop him for the NBA. Earvin finally bought into Payne's sales pitch and that was that.

The night before Earvin's long awaited announcement, Jud appeared at a dinner at Walnut Hills Country Club. I tried to read his expressions and I misread him. He looked calm enough but he didn't look happy enough. He claimed he didn't know which way Earvin would go the next day, but of course he already knew he had his prized recruit.

Earvin's news conference began at 9 a.m. in the school auditorium. There were media people from everywhere in attendance. His announcement was carried live over the school public address system, but nowhere else. As soon as he said "Michigan State" I ran down the hall and grabbed the nearest pay phone. I called my office and we got it on radio and television as fast as we could.

That afternoon, I walked into Hal Gross' office with a suggestion.

"We should broadcast his games at Michigan State," I told him.

"I agree," he said. "We can sell a good radio package."

"No. I'm talking television," I went on. "They're going to sell out all these games next season and people will want to see him play. We've already done his one high school game—let's do as many as we can next season."

In those days there were no cable outlets and no TV basketball packages for each school, at least not at Michigan State. There were no rights fees either. Michigan State officials thought we were doing the school a favor by carrying a number of games—it would remove some of the ticket pressure.

We made an agreement to carry about ten games for each of two seasons. Coincidentally, Earvin stayed for two years. We put our director, Joe Murphy, on the project and we aired these games with our own production personnel.

Today, production companies use huge trucks to satellite games to their various stations. In those days we were like Thomas Edison creating the light bulb. We never went off the air, which we were proud of and we had few on-air glitches. The station made a ton of money and we all had a lot of fun. We carried several Big Ten road games.

I thought the Spartans might have won the national championship in Earvin's freshman year. There was no shot clock that season and so the team didn't have to run if it didn't want to play that way. Michigan State lost in the NCAA tournament to Kentucky, 52-49, in Dayton. It was a game I thought the Spartans would have won if they'd just turned their offense loose. It was not to be.

The next year they nearly had a team mutiny after going 4-4 through the first portion of the Big Ten schedule. The players and coaches had a serious meeting at that point and Jud altered his strategy a bit from that time on.

Imagine a team with all the talent those Spartans had, losing at Northwestern, 83-65. But they did and it may have been a blessing in disguise. Their only loss from that time forward was the result of a mid court buzzer beater shot at Wisconsin. They shared the Big Ten title with Iowa and Purdue at 13-5, but they were clearly the team to beat in the NCAA tournament.

I did not go to Salt Lake City for the Final Four because our network did not carry the MSU games. It also would have been very expensive to try and send stories back, so the station saved the money.

But when the team arrived back home I was at Jenison with a live TV hook up for the celebration. We wiped out the entire six o'clock news to carry the pandemonium. I also helped organize a victory parade down Michigan Avenue. It was an event unlike the city had ever seen before or has since.

On a cold, windy day, with bands leading the way, the Spartans paraded from the Frandor Shopping Center to the State Capitol. They sat atop convertibles and Earvin and Greg Kelser rode in the last car. The crowd mobbed them to the point that they could barely get inside the State Capitol building for another presentation. Thousands of people swarmed them and I think they both feared for their own safety. It was truly an incredible scene.

Earvin played for two distinctly different coaches in high school and college. George Fox knew how to shmooze him just the right way, but he would not put up with any tardiness either. One night the Everett bus was leaving for a road game and Earvin had not yet arrived. Fox warned his dad: "If he's not there, we're leaving without him." Earvin just made it and he was never close to being late again.

Jud was careful with him also and he listened to Earvin's suggestions. Their relationship grew and so did their respect for each other. They didn't always agree, but they knew they needed each other to be successful.

As Earvin always likes to say: "When I was in the NBA I had the green light to shoot—when I played for Jud I had the caution light."

Soon after winning the national championship, Earvin declared for the NBA draft and so his tenure in mid-Michigan came to an end. The community was almost out of breath from following his every move on a basketball court for five years. It was an era that many fans will never forget and neither will I.

Since I broadcast so many of his games, I became friends not only with Earvin, but his parents also. If you know Earvin's parents, you know why he is as polite and gracious as he is. Earvin, Sr., and Christine Johnson are lovely people and you've probably heard their famous son praise them at many public events. They love all of their children and they are guided by their religious faith. Earvin idolizes his father and praises his mother to anyone who will listen. All of them had to learn how to live with the celebrity of "Magic Johnson," and they were never really comfortable in the public eye, even to this day.

After his rookie NBA season, I invited Earvin to my home for dinner with his girlfriend. It was the summer of 1980 and I told him, "Don't drive some fancy car with the top down into my neighborhood—the kids will see you and then we won't have any privacy."

So here comes Earvin, with the top down in a gorgeous Mercedes, on a warm night with kids playing in the street. Fifteen minutes later, I must have had 50 kids in my yard, all of whom wanted to meet him. Dinner was fine, but we had to lock all the doors.

Later that summer, I asked him to help me with some on-air television promos about my move to WILX-TV. We met at Everett High School one afternoon and spent more than an hour shooting a variety of commercials. There was no payment to him for this and he did a great job. We had a lot of fun and I still have the outtakes reel to this day.

Several years later, I was the subject of a "roast" to benefit the Special Olympics. Earvin agreed to be one of the "roasters," but he would be coming in from an appearance in the Bahamas. We advertised him as one of the speakers and that helped to sell tickets. We had not heard from him in the days leading up to the event, but the morning of the roast he called me.

"Don't worry. I'll be there," he promised.

If you know Earvin, you know he is rarely on time for anything. But he walked in by himself midway through dinner and the evening turned out great. He was very funny and he enjoyed himself. Jud was part of the program also and they took some great shots at me and at each other. Earvin likes to tease me to others about my prediction that he would end up at Michigan. That isn't really true, but I never correct him, because he always enjoys embellishing that story.

On Thanksgiving, 1986, he invited Cathy and me, along with our friends, Phil and Judy Kurth and their two daughters, to visit him in Los Angeles. It would be a four-day trip we will never forget. Earvin's agent at the time, Charles Tucker, who still works out of Lansing, set up everything for us, from our hotel rooms to our rental car. I got us Thanksgiving night tickets to the Tonight Show with Johnny Carson. David Letterman was his guest that night and the two of them made it a memorable evening. Letterman, of course, had not yet joined CBS.

The next night we were to attend the Lakers game with the

Chicago Bulls and their prized rookie, Michael Jordan. The Bulls were staying at the same hotel we were and leaving the next morning. We literally bumped into Jordan coming down the elevator. Kristen Kurth was living in Chicago at the time and introduced herself.

"Can I have my picture taken with you?" she asked Jordan.

"Okay, but only if you don't tell your boyfriend," he told her with a smile. We were all impressed, but Michael Jordan in 1986 was not yet the Michael Jordan of today.

I was nervous about the arrangements to pick up our tickets that night so we went to the Forum in the morning to see Earvin at the Lakers' shoot-around. I informed the guard at the tunnel entrance who I was and who I wanted to see.

Of course he had never heard of Tim Staudt, but no one ever called Magic Johnson, Earvin Johnson. He did notice that I had a Michigan driver's license.

"Wait here and let me see what I can find out," he said.

Fifteen minutes later, up the tunnel entrance with the guard, walked Earvin. Time for handshakes and hugs and introductions with all of my party. At that time, other fans in the parking lot swarmed around him for an autograph.

"Everybody step back," he barked. "These are friends from back home. I'll get to all of you in a few moments."

We agreed to meet after the game. Earvin's buddy, Darwin Payton, would take Phil and me into the locker room. Darwin was the MSU team manager during the national championship season and Earvin gave him a full time job managing some of his affairs in Los Angeles.

The Lakers won and Phil and I got to meet some of the Lakers. The Kurth girls recognized Rob Lowe in the stands and were more impressed seeing him than the players.

The next day we agreed to visit Earvin's home in Beverly Hills.

"Come at three o'clock," he ordered. "I want you to see my sunset. Just drive up to the gate and tell the guard who you are."

We had rented a station wagon and we looked like tourists driving up to this glitzy neighborhood. I rolled down the window as the gate keeper stopped us.

"My name's Tim Staudt. We are here to visit Earvin Johnson."

Once again, a dubious look. We were waved through after a phone call and at the top of a hill about a quarter mile away, we arrived in bachelor Earvin Johnson's driveway. He and Darwin were on the front lawn to greet us.

We got the grand tour and this mansion would have made Hugh Hefner blush. He had a card room, a full sized gymnasium and a gorgeous kitchen. He had five bedrooms. The house was decorated spectacularly and it was as clean as can be because of his hired help.

He had a walk-in closet the size of a bedroom itself. And the view out the back over the swimming pool was everything he promised. It looked down into a long gorge toward some mountains. The sunset was indeed impressive.

We stayed several hours and as we left I thought back to those days at Everett High School just ten short years before. Who would ever have known, let alone Earvin, that this was the course his life would take. What an incredible story.

We see each other several times a year whenever he is in town. I have emceed his golf outings and we have visited at his parents' home. He has moved them twice since he became an NBA player. I have always told him that I would never fight the multitudes of people in his life for personal time together. When we see each other it is special even though those times are fewer as the years go by.

Greg Kelser drove home with me one night after a basketball game last season in Columbus, Ohio.

"Do you have people try to use you as a pipeline to Earvin?" he asked me.

"Why do you?" I answered with a question.

"All the time. And you know I can't do it. I am not a pipeline to him. It is hard enough for me to get through to him."

I've often told Earvin over the years that he has no idea how many fans I have screened from him. Every charity around who wants either a jersey, an autograph, or an appearance from him figures I can pull that off or certainly help try to seal a deal. I rarely try because I know what the chances of success are. Earvin just doesn't have enough time. Kelser alluded to the same problem.

When Earvin announced he was getting married, I figured I wouldn't believe it until I saw it. I had met Cookie several times before when they were dating. My wife liked her immediately and we both felt Earvin was lucky that she waited around for him. She would be getting into a difficult lifestyle because of the demands on his time. When it was announced that the wedding would take place in Lansing in September, 1991, my wife asked if we'd be getting an invitation. I had no idea what to think.

There was a great deal of media speculation about the wedding because of who might attend. Would Jack Nicholson show up? What about other NBA stars? What about Dyan Cannon? There were many other Hollywood celebrities who were friendly with Earvin and the public got all excited. I knew he wasn't about to try and drag all those people to his hometown, but I didn't really know what his plans were.

The wedding would take place in the evening on a Saturday. It was the same day Michigan State hosted Central Michigan in football. I woke up that morning figuring I'd cover the football game and watch coverage of Earvin's wedding later that night on the local news. Then the phone rang with a sleepy voice on the other end.

"Tim, this is Earvin. Did my mother call you and invite you to the wedding?"

"No, no one has called me."

"I can't believe that," he said. "You and your wife are on the guest list. I'm at the Sheraton. Can you come over and pick up a pass? You'll need it to get into the parking lot of the church. The wedding is at six o'clock and you can't be late."

"That's funny coming from you," I told him. "Will you be on time?"

When I told Cathy we were invited to the wedding that night I thought her eyes would fall out of her head. She immediately got her camera ready and borrowed a dress from a friend. I went to the football game— the Spartans lost—but my mind was on the wedding that night.

I did not know where the Union Missionary Baptist Church was. I knew I was in the right location when I arrived because of all the police and several hundred spectators on the site hoping to catch a glimpse of the proceedings. Before we were seated I looked for the men's room in the basement. I noticed Earvin down the hall pacing nervously with his family alongside.

The wedding began promptly at six and it had all the whistles and bells. Isiah Thomas and Mark Aguirre were among the groomsmen. I didn't recognize many of the guests—most were family who had traveled from out of state. The service lasted about 45 minutes and when we stepped outside the church there were people cheering for as far as I could see. I wanted to leave for the Kellogg Center reception as quickly as I could so as to beat the crowd, which would soon move to that location. A roar went up when Earvin and Cookie emerged from the church.

The reception was a closely guarded affair and I've never seen the Big Ten room look quite that glamorous. It was completely made over. In the receiving line I whispered to Cookie:

"You must be exhausted by now."

"No, this is the night I've been waiting for all my life," she smiled back. And she certainly did look very happy. After three hours and several hundred pictures we left with the bride and groom still busy dancing the night away. Earvin was having the time of his life. No one knew then that his world would turn upside down less than two months later.

I was standing in the WILX-TV newsroom in Jackson that day in November when the phone rang in my office. It was a producer from our NBC affiliate in Detroit on the other end of the line.

"Have you heard the news about Magic Johnson?" he asked. "There are rumors he has AIDS and he is going to retire from the NBA this afternoon."

That was too much for me to focus on all at once. My mind simply could not comprehend what I was being told. A few minutes later, our wire machine reported that the Lakers had called an important news conference in one hour.

By the end of that day, I had fielded nearly 100 phone calls and I had aired a live, 30-minute special on Earvin Johnson that night at 11:30. I called his home during the evening to wish him my best and Darwin answered. They were all having dinner.

"I don't want to bother him," I said. "Just tell him and Cookie I called and they are in Cathy's and my prayers."

"I will," Darwin said. "And he'll appreciate it."

Last spring I sat down with Earvin while he was working out at the Michigan Athletic Club in East Lansing. He was home for a few days. I couldn't believe how good he looked. Had this guy actually beaten the dreaded HIV virus? He never looked stronger and at age 38, he played basketball up and down the court for more than an hour with all the bounce that he enjoyed during his glory days in the NBA.

Earvin has a will and a resolve that I have found in few other people. He was determined to lick his disease to make sure he would be around for his family. He is convinced he is cured. He has worked like the dickens to keep himself in tip-top shape. He is much more appreciative of how good life has been to him than perhaps he was when he was a star player.

I always tell him, "Earvin when people ask me about you and my favorite memories, I don't talk about the NBA and I don't talk about Michigan State. I think back to those early days when you were in high school, before the world knew who you were. Those are my favorite memories that are different from how most others remember you." And that's how I truly feel.

At one time, I evaluated him as the greatest player who ever lived. Today, perhaps a bit more objectively, I call him one of the five greatest. I also add that he may be the greatest winner the game has ever produced. Winning was something he instilled in all those around him at every level of the game. He played on a state championship high school team, an NCAA championship college team and five NBA title-winning teams. Not bad.

He obviously has been the highlight individual of my career. He has driven me crazy over the years trying to track him down for interviews when he has been in town. Too many people want a piece of his time. It has always seemed to be that way.

The private times have always been special for me. I will never forget all those games I broadcast and the images of his spectacular play will forever be etched in my memory. He has given so many of us many magical moments.

Swing and a miss. Sometimes you gotta get out there and take your knocks.

A young journalist in 1973...

The biggest scoop for me ever was announcing Duffy was stepping down.

with Duffy Daugherty
Jan. 23, 1979

Magic and I enjoy a day at the course.

In my profession I've been blessed to meet many
international superstars like Arthur Ashe.

Spartan great Steve Garvey.

I've always enjoyed radio work, especially with people like George Blaha.

Bobby Riggs is quite the entertainer.

A well-dressed WJIM TV-6 Sports Reporter.

So much of the work in our business is done behind the cameras; Eric Hess does a marvelous job for NBC 10.

In our business, we work as a team to become successful.

Looking back over thirty years, I feel a great sense of
satisfaction and pride for bringing you the stories.

Chapter 10

People

I've met many interesting people in the last 30 years. You have already read about a number of them. In no particular order, here are some thoughts on others of note I've come across.

JIM DELANY. He is the Big Ten Commissioner. He took over for Wayne Duke in 1989. Bo Schembechler doesn't like him —he thinks he is too basketball-oriented. Delany came down hard on Bo when he misbehaved on the sidelines. I like Delany. He is a tough negotiator and I believe he has the Big Ten's best interests at heart. He formed the league's lucrative TV packages. He is cautious in what he says publicly, but he is a bright guy who understands the big-time college sports business. I believe Delany would be a good baseball commissioner, except that he would never take a job with so little authority.

JOE FALLS. I met Joe on the infield of Tiger Stadium back in 1968. Curt Sylvester of the Free Press introduced us. From that day forward Joe has been a good friend. I have always felt his writing skills were superb. He is in his late 60s now and his health has been shaky at times. But he still has a passion to write. He has struggled to maintain his journalistic clout in Detroit because the newspaper management there has turned over so many times and some of them haven't had a clue about how to use him properly.

Joe is always accused of being anti-Michigan State. He is not, but I do not argue on his behalf anymore and he rarely argues this issue either. He can't win. People think what they think. When the school went through countless controversies in the '70s and '80s, Joe commented on them. Because it wasn't all positive, hard core fans called him unfairly negative. He has been a Godsend to the Michigan Special Olympics, helping raise millions of dollars for the cause. We talk often and I try to inform him on Michigan State issues if he asks and if I think I have some inside dope.

The public will never appreciate his career when he's gone. He was hired to write opinions and stir up people's interest. Over the years, in that regard, I believe he grades an A. Sports fans around Michigan have all read Joe Falls at one time or another— he was successful because he stirred up their passions on various issues. He came to Michigan in 1953. He must have done something right to last in his business that long.

MIKE DITKA. I emceed a dinner in Lansing several years ago when Ditka worked for NBC sports and was fresh from his coaching with the Chicago Bears. He was the speaker and was pleasant and funny. Ditka told the audience, "Now I'm in the media, so I've got all the answers." They laughed. He is a principled guy and today's athletes, like those he has on the New Orleans Saints, must drive him crazy with their contemporary values.

BOBBY BOWDEN. Every coach in America should hear this guy speak. I introduced him at a banquet in Lansing in the spring of 1997. He was fabulous. His record at Florida State is spectacular. He can flat-out sell because he has such a warm personality. Bowden is humorous in the style of Duffy Daugherty and he has parlayed that talent into a huge outside income. Bowden told me he never hires assistant coaches who don't want to become head coaches. He wants them hungry and competing amongst themselves to win his favor. That way they know he'll recommend them for head coaching jobs of their own. I love Bowden's creative offensive genius. No one gets bored watching Florida State play. Of course he has great athletes, but he knows how to use a warm, down home personality to win recruits and their parents over to his side.

ARTHUR ASHE. I introduced him at a tennis benefit held at Lansing Eastern High School's fieldhouse back in the 1970s. He could still play extremely well and his thoughtful demeanor was impressive. What a tragedy that he died so young. Ashe could have run for political office and won because he had high credibility. He was a serious guy, but I could tell people listened to what he had to say very closely.

BOBBY RIGGS. He made his fame when he played Billy Jean King in Houston. We brought him to Lansing for a tennis benefit against local Dr. Thomas Jamieson in 1978. Jamieson is known for his golfing talent, but he was a superb tennis player in his day. Jamieson gave Riggs the doubles court and he took the singles area only for an exhibition charity match at Lansing Eastern High School one night. The place was packed. Riggs beat Tom to a pulp with that kind of an advantage, although Jamieson acquitted himself very well.

Riggs loved golf and they lined him up with a big stakes game earlier in the day at the Country Club of Lansing. They snookered him good with some local rule calls and he wasn't too happy about losing several hundred dollars. He was kind of kooky but he was fun to be around.

FRANK BECKMANN. He founded Sportsrap on WJR and I wish he was still the host. Hosting Sportsrap gave Frank a huge forum every night and access to great and timely guests. When Ernie Harwell left the Tigers' radio booth, Frank moved in for an increase in pay. That part makes sense. But traveling all over the place for 162 games plus spring training to follow a team that has modest interest and may well never contend for a pennant surprised me. Frank loves to play golf around Michigan and he had many great opportunities with his original assignment. He also could stay close to the University of Michigan which he loves. Now he only calls the Michigan games during a portion of the football season. The Tigers couldn't pay me enough money to do their radio play-by-play. But Frank apparently likes it. I do miss him on Sportsrap however—he never fought with the callers as others do.

JIM BRANDSTATTER. Mr. Michigan. When I was a senior at East Lansing High School in 1967, Jim was a junior. He was the first baseman on our baseball team. He could hit with power, but I'm sure even he'd admit he lacked foot speed on the bases. I pitched and he'd even admit again that I had a pretty successful senior year.

Jim used to anchor the sports at WILX-TV back in the early 1970s when the studios were in Jackson. There he met his wife, Robbie Timmons, currently the anchor at WXYZ-TV in Detroit. She's an Ohio Stater so they have lively conversations the week of the big game each November. Jim came from a great athletic family, beginning with his dad, Art Sr. He was a superb football player at Michigan State. Art, Jr., later played end for Duffy Daugherty in the late '50s. I believe Art, Jr., may have been the greatest over-all high school athlete ever to come out of the mid-Michigan area.

ERNIE HARWELL. In an era when most media people are never considered heroes in the eyes of the public, Ernie Harwell is an exception. I've watched large groups of people line up to buy his books and have him autograph them. Ernie truly is a nice guy. He adapted to baseball's changing from a sport to mostly a business. Ernie is a devout Christian and not afraid to tell it to anyone. He has always been thankful for what he's had in life, especially his good health. Ernie is a very upbeat guy and that's why he continues to broadcast today, in the twilight of his life.

SPARKY ANDERSON. I had never really met Sparky personally until I emceed a banquet in Lansing where he was the speaker. This was a kids benefit and Sparky was late arriving because of traffic in the Detroit area. He brought his wife and they sat at a table in the audience with me and a host of other kids. Sparky could not have been nicer to them. The Tigers had a rare off day, but Sparky didn't seem put-out about spending it on the road for a speech. He carefully spoke with as many kids as he could and he stayed well past his talk to sign autographs and talk with parents. He was paid for the appearance, but he gave them their money's worth. His message was upbeat and friendly and I wrote him a note afterward telling him how much I thought he positively affected those kids' lives that night.

FUZZY ZOELLER. Maybe the nicest guy on the pro golf tour. Never mind the Tiger Woods controversy, Fuzzy is as good as they come. He represented Oldsmobile for awhile and he came to Lansing for an appearance to help raise money for a kid hit by lightning. This was a couple of years ago. I emceed the evening, dubbed "An Evening with Fuzzy Zoeller." He didn't spend much time with his speech, but he mingled with everyone in attendance and he was great with the handicapped youngster.

That summer, at the Buick Open in Grand Blanc, I found him drinking a beer with the fans at the grill after one of his rounds instead of going inside to the nicer players' room. He recognized me and we talked for awhile. Fuzzy is genuine. He doesn't "big time" it and his attitude on the course could be more closely emulated by amateurs who play.

SCOTTY BOWMAN. I'd heard he was tough to deal with and maybe he is at times. But one night I hosted a live one-hour hockey special from a restaurant Ron Mason partly owned. Ron and Scotty are friends. We had a large audience and Scotty drove up from Detroit on a night off. This show, of course, featured the winningest coach in NHL history and the winningest coach in college history. Scotty could not have been nicer and I challenged them to some hockey trivial pursuit, which they did not know about beforehand. Scotty was pretty good, too. Ron thinks the world of him and he sure gave a great evening of hockey entertainment that night.

DICK VITALE. I claim this guy is one of the greatest success stories in the history of sportscasting. He was a balding, one-eyed coach who was fired by the Detroit Pistons, when broadcasting became his next option. Who could ever have imagined that this guy would forever change the public's vision of the college game. He is arguably the biggest celebrity in college basketball and he is mobbed for interviews wherever he goes.

Dick is a very genuine person. I first met him in 1977. I did the TV play-by-play of Michigan State's basketball game at Detroit, where Dick was athletic director. Gus Ganakas worked the game with me and we stopped down early in the day to visit with him. He still wasn't "Dick Vitale" at this time of course, but Gus knew and liked him. Vitale was funny and never stopped talking, just like today. When we left his office I told Gus "my ears are hoarse." Gus hasn't stopped laughing over that line.

At the game that night, Detroit had a wild opening ceremony to introduce its players and Vitale thought it up. It featured lights, music and smoke, much the way NBA teams are introduced today. The place was packed. Earvin and the guys blew the Titans out of the gym.

When Vitale became coach of the Pistons, his team played an exhibition game at the Lansing Civic Center. That night, I sat at press row absolutely adjacent to the Pistons' bench so I could hear every word he offered during time-outs.

"Hubbard, will you start playing some defense," he screamed at former Michigan star Phil Hubbard. "You guys are not going to get me fired because you refuse to play defense." Eventually their lack of defense and other problems did cause Dick to get fired.

When a close friend of mine turned 50 years old a few years ago I spent six months assembling a video to wish him happy birthday. It featured celebrities offering him birthday congratulations. Vitale was in Lansing to make a speech and I asked him to help me out. He gave me two minutes of his best Dickie V stuff. While I had many other celebrities on that tape, Vitale's stuff was tops.

He lives in Sarasota, Florida, where my parents live in the wintertime so we touch base whenever we happen to be in town at the same time. Dick is always sending my kids the various basketball items he is endorsing and it always comes in a huge box. I can only imagine the annual income he is raking in today and it's a far cry from his days as just one more fired NBA coach. Vitale is smart enough to know that treating everyone with friendliness can only help him. People gravitate to him and he isn't put off by that. When he does a game, he literally becomes a major added attraction in the arena that night. ESPN was smart enough to lock him into a seven-year contract extension earlier this year. For a few more years anyway he'll continue to be a prime time player.

Several years ago he worked a game at the Breslin Center and I did my 6 p.m. sportscast at his hotel downtown. I didn't get into all the serious pre-game stuff and he gave me three and a half minutes of pure shtick. My final question was: "If I was playing in the game tonight and you were doing the play-by-play, how would it sound if I made a great play to win it?"

He never missed a beat though he didn't know the question was coming.

"Well Timmy Staudt dribbles into the corner, he dishes the rock off to the big guy inside, then he takes the return pass behind the arc." His eyes are as big as saucers and he's gesturing wildly into the camera at this point. I'm sitting there laughing like crazy.

"The clock is winding down—he squares up and shoots the pill—oh! oh!, nothing but net, baby! He's supah! He's sensational! He's a prime-time player—a Rolls Roycer. He's more than just a member of my all-airport team!"

By this time, the people in the lobby had assembled to watch this act and everyone was laughing wildly. It was great stuff. When Dick's around you don't need a whole lot of substance, you just need more air time. And he asked for it.

"Oh they're wrapping us up," he groaned. "I want more air

time, I want more air time." They just faded to commercial and Dick shook hands and left for the Breslin Center.

BRENT MUSBURGER. He had it all when he was hosting the NFL Today on CBS. Then he got into the contract fiasco with the network over whether he'd host the Olympic games. So they fired him, nearly on the spot. He barely got to finish the NCAA basketball tournament. The lesson to be learned is that no matter how big you are, or think you are, you can always be replaced.

Brent has been nice to me. He knew my dad really well. My dad dished out those Chevrolet Scholarships after all the college football games on television. He'd travel around the country to the big games to do it and he got to meet a lot of network people. He has a picture in his Charlevoix summer home of Brent and him sitting on the CBS Sports set in New York.

ABC kicked him off the golf telecasts and I thought his big problem was that he made it sound like a football game without the crowd noise. Who knows how his career might have ended up had he not infuriated the CBS management over that contract demand.

WOODY HAYES. I worked for six years while Woody was still the coach of the Buckeyes. Whenever he came to town it was a big event. He was occasionally approachable, but that was on Friday before the game at the Buckeyes' practice in Spartan Stadium. The rivalry, in my judgment, with Michigan is not the same with Woody and Bo gone. They were the stars, they were the celebrities. You tended to watch them on the sidelines almost as much as the action on the field.

In 1965, when I was in high school, the Buckeyes were staying at the old Albert Pick Motor Hotel in East Lansing the night before their game with the Spartans. Saturday morning broke bright with sunshine and warm temperatures. We lived several blocks from the Albert Pick. We had friends from Ohio visiting that weekend.

After breakfast, I looked out our living room window and was stunned by what I saw. I thought I was actually dreaming. There was Woody, in his customary short-sleeve white shirt and tie, walking his players through the neighborhood just to get some exercise and while away the time. The Buckeyes all wore their gray blazers, with close cropped haircuts and they had stony looks on their faces. I screamed for the family to look. Here we are with all of our noses pressed up against the windows to watch the Buckeyes casually walking through an East Lansing neighborhood. It would be the best part of their day.

Michigan State clobbered them 32-7 and held the Buckeyes to negative yards rushing.

NANCY LOPEZ. I met her in 1976 when Michigan State hosted the women's national collegiate golf championship. There were no NCAA women's sports then—the governing body was the AIAW—the Association of Intercollegiate Athletics for Women. The whole community got involved in staging the tournament. Nancy was in the field representing her University of Tulsa team.

She had been playing in England and flew in just before the first round. She was just beginning to make a name for herself. That tournament featured a number of future LPGA players including Beth Daniel and Betsy King. Lopez hit the ball further than all of them and she drew the biggest gallery. She caught Barb Barrow of Stanford in the final holes and then defeated her in a play-off with a birdie on the fourth hole. She was very gracious in victory.

Her star quality gave the LPGA a much-needed boost, but since she has become a mother and wife her priorities, of course, have changed. The LPGA still has not replaced Nancy Lopez' celebrity. She is still just about the biggest draw on tour even though her game isn't what it once was.

When she represented Oldsmobile, she came to East Lansing for the Oldsmobile Classic. That gave the tournament a boost. When she was dropped as a client, she dropped the tournament and has not been back. Such is the business of pro sports.

ROGER PENSKE. I met him through my dad. In the late '70s my dad brought him to the American Cancer Society pro am tournament in Lansing, but he wasn't nearly the big name then that he is today. Penske obviously has been a tremendous force in auto racing. He has a bright vision, he thinks big and he is well organized. He took the Michigan International Speedway and bought it at a time when it was about to go out of business. Now it is one of the premier tracks in the country. Penske would be successful in just about anything. He demands much from his employees, but he gets production because of that attitude. I've interviewed him on several occasions during the pro am golf tournament before the Michigan 500 auto race in Jackson. He always has something to say and he is very pleasant.

CHARLES KURALT. He may have been the greatest story teller in the history of television news. And if he isn't, then I do not know who is. Anyone in broadcasting can learn from what Charles Kuralt did. He wasn't the best looking guy, but he sure knew how to tell stories and get people's attention. He was a very pleasant man. I met him when he stopped through Lansing en route to one of his On the Road features. WJIM-TV, being a CBS affiliate, was a station he could stop and visit while passing through. He had his camera man with him and he stayed for about an hour visiting with our management. He told us how he looked for his various feature stories and we were all captivated. What a great talent.

WAYNE FONTES. Over my career, he was the most maligned coach in the history of sports in this state. And I can't think of anyone else who would even be a close second. I saw Wayne in December, 1997, at a Michigan State basketball game in Tampa against South Florida.

He walked in with a friend and he looked great. He told me he had lost 42 pounds and had joined an area country club. He smiled and signed numerous autographs for the fans sitting nearby.

Wayne was an excellent second baseman for the Spartans' baseball team. He also played defensive back for Duffy Daugherty and he has remained loyal to Michigan State. He is a good friend of George Perles and they visited frequently when both were coaching together.

"I don't miss it at all," he told me a year ago when I asked him about coaching the Lions. "I have a lot less stress!"

AL KALINE. I loved watching him play for the Tigers when I grew up because he was very consistent. I like his work as a broadcaster because he tells it like it is, but he does so without being antagonistic. You can tell that he gets fed up with some of today's players. His sons used to work for WILX-TV when I was at WJIM. Both have since left television.

Al loves golf and is a very good player at Oakland Hills Country Club in Birmingham. I bump into him occasionally at various outings and he is very agreeable to interviews and he enjoys conversation. The game would be much better off today if

Al Kaline could dictate exactly how it would be run and how the players would conduct themselves.

J.P. McCARTHY. In August, 1995, I was vacationing with the family in Frankfort. The phone rang and it was my assistant, Eric Hess, with the news.

"I thought you'd want to know," he began. "J.P. McCarthy died today."

I was absolutely stunned. I knew he was off the air and he was ill, but J.P. was about as immortal as they come. How would the people of Detroit ever deal with this? How would WJR ever deal with it? I couldn't imagine driving around in the morning without listening to J.P.

This guy was one of the greatest broadcast talents I'd ever met. I knew him because he played golf with my dad from time to time. He was very helpful with suggestions to me about my own career. I studied his interviewing techniques very closely for years. It amazed me how he could ask tough questions to coaches and they wouldn't get upset. The same questions asked by someone else would send the same coaches into a rage.

J.P. knew how to succeed in broadcasting. He knew that becoming friendly with big-time sports celebrities could only help him. He knew everyone around Detroit and he was friendly with them all. They trusted him to give them a fair shake and so most were almost eager to be interviewed on his show.

When all the major Detroit television stations carried his funeral live, you knew this guy was a vital part of the community. I miss listening to him to this day. I learned as much about broadcasting just listening to him as I have from anyone. I also learned that there are many advantages to treating people the way he did. No one was too big to say no to being a guest on J.P.'s show, from the President of the United States right on down.

HAROLD F. GROSS. Most of you do not know who this man is. He turned 97 this last summer as I write this. He founded Gross Telecasting, Inc., which produced the area's first television station, WJIM-TV. He took great pride in having the famed Country House built in 1954, just west of the Frandor Shopping Center. He was the sole owner of the station and its radio sister.

I worked for him through the decade of the '70s. He gave me my first chance in television. In a way he was like a second father to me, but he was not an easy boss. Whereas we had many good times together, he demanded a lot from his employees. Some bought into his firm ways and others could not. His firm methods made it much easier for me to deal with other bosses down the road.

Gross was a pioneer, therefore he was used to doing things his way. He was not a liberated individual. He fought off a union challenge in the mid 1970s. His broadcast license was challenged in the later years of his ownership which eventually led him to selling his stations and retiring from the business.

Hal Gross loaned me money interest-free to buy my first home. He hosted a bachelor dinner for me and it was a fabulous affair. He got to know the rest of my family on a social basis. I did not feel good about leaving him for the station's competitor, WILX-TV, in 1980.

I'd been thinking about making a move for a year simply because I decided that if I was to grow professionally and financially, I would need to move on to a broader opportunity. When the newspaper learned that I was negotiating to leave it made front page headlines. That was the first Gross learned that I was debating a move. He tried to talk me out of it but by then I was pretty set in my mind that I was going to leave. His friends called and told me to stay put. Still, I was convinced I'd go. I signed my contract and then had to face him.

I called him one morning and asked to come visit and he knew what this was all about. He heard me out and I didn't elaborate. He was angry and felt I'd betrayed him, but I left in a hurry so as not to belabor the situation. In time, we remained friends and I nearly returned to the station in 1982. He made a competitive offer to me, but I felt that he would soon leave the business because of his age and then I wouldn't know who my boss would be.

Over the past ten years I have visited his East Lansing home on a regular basis for morning coffee. I always update him on the state of the industry, which leads him to start shaking his head in disbelief.

"I'm glad I got out when I did," he always reminds me.

Hal Gross has a penchant for living that I have seen in few other people. He struggled with his health a few years ago and he has been confined to a wheelchair. At the time it left him depressed, but he has now adapted well. He is not "retired" in the truest sense. He conducts business from his home. He is involved with many investments and he makes numerous charitable contributions. He donated the funds which built the home for the lions and tigers at Lansing's Potter Park Zoo. He has a tremendous zest for living and he gets the most out of each day. His mind is still very sharp. I can't fool him like I did when he first employed me.

I don't know if I ever would have made it in this business had Hal Gross not given me my first chance. I had high respect for him as an employer then and I always will.

MARTHA DIXON. The most loyal friend I had through my Channel 6 years was Martha Dixon. She is in her mid 70s now and I still visit with her several times a year. She has a home in East Lansing and also on Sanibel Island in Florida. Growing in your profession when you are only in your 20s can cause plenty of stress. Martha helped me through many rough times with her guidance. She was a superb on-air talent. She hosted a woman's show, live, called The Copper Kettle, which was very famous and successful back in the '50s and '60s. She anchored some other shows and I co-hosted several of them with her, including the Labor Day Jerry Lewis Telethon. I can still say to this day that Martha Dixon is the finest on-air television professional with whom I have ever worked. Viewers loved her and she was very genuine. Her faith is important to her and she has a compassion for others. She was a spectacular salesperson at the station, too. Martha Dixon was the MVP of WJIM-TV as far as I'm concerned.

RON MASON. It's quite an accomplishment to be the all-time winningest coach in your sport. Ron Mason, in his late 50s, still shows great enthusiasm for the game and his job. I have hosted his television show the past few years and I detect no signs of burnout. He loves it as much today as he ever has. Ron was smart enough to stay away from the NHL and the insecurity that goes with a coach's life in the pros. He knew Michigan State was a perfect fit for him and he has made the most of it.

For awhile he was mentioned as a great candidate to become athletic director and he'd have been good at it because he knows college sports and he is good with people. But his love for coaching has never subsided to the point where he wanted to make that change. He has high credibility with everyone in hockey.

He kids about being left alone in the bowels of Munn Arena by all the powers that be at the university. That is probably more truth than fiction in terms of his remaining happy as the coach of the Spartans.

He became honorary chairman of the Children's Miracle Network for Sparrow Hospital when it was founded in 1989 and has stayed with it ever since. CMN has profited greatly from his participation. Ron is an excellent ad lib speaker with a good sense of humor. He plays well to television and he is one of the few coaches around today who could host his own television show successfully without a host to toss him questions.

Of all the on-air comments I've made over the years, one about Ron is one I wish I could have taken back. As soon as he was named to replace Amo Bessone, I criticized him on air for not attending the team banquet to help say good-bye to Amo. I don't know why that was such a big deal to me at the time, but here the guy hadn't even been on the job yet and the local TV guy was criticizing him. I wish I could forget that night, but I can't. Sorry Ron.

GREG KELSER. Everyone who meets Greg likes him and it's easy to see why. He is nice to everyone, laid back and friendly. I've worked eight seasons of Big Ten television basketball with him and we've had some great times together. Greg works many more games during a season than I do—it's his main job.

He travels all over the place and just as when he played, he carefully makes sure he rests the afternoon before night games by taking a nap in his hotel room.

Traveling through the Midwest in the winter is hazardous because of the weather and we've had some strange journeys to broadcast these games.

In 1996, we were scheduled to go to Madison to work the Michigan State at Wisconsin game. We almost never travel together because we leave from different locations. On that day, I drove with a friend the morning of the game which I often do when the travel time is five hours or less. After an hour on the road, Greg called me on my car phone.

"I'm stranded at Metro Airport in Detroit," he said. "Can you wait in Kalamazoo and drive us the rest of the way if I can make it there in a couple of hours on a flight?"

I told him I better keep going because one of us had to get there. He finally agreed.

"I'll get there some way." He eventually rented a car and

drove the six hours before leaving his car off at the Madison Airport. He took a cab to the game and made it with an hour to spare, pretty exhausted from an already long day.

After working the game he flew home with the MSU team and his wife drove from their Farmington Hills home to pick him up in Lansing. All in all, not an easy day.

During the 1997 season he talked the Big Ten into letting him work a doubleheader. He would call a noon game at Indiana, then be driven to Indianapolis to catch at flight to Detroit. From there he planned to drive to the Breslin Center and work an MSU game with me that night. It was a good plan if he encountered no delays. At four o'clock that afternoon, I got a call at home.

"I'm stranded at Indianapolis because of the the weather," he told me. "Tell the producer I'll make it eventually. If you can, try to keep them from finding a replacement."

If I could convince the Big Ten people that I could work the game solo, then he would get paid for the second game if he could make it for even a portion of the telecast. Our producer tried to find a replacement, but came up empty because of the short notice.

"Don't worry, I can do this alone, I've done it before." Without much other choice I went on the air as play-by-play and color man all wrapped into one. I did not explain Greg's plight on the air—other announcers have worked solo, so by not calling attention to it we figured maybe the audience wouldn't notice.

With ten minutes to play in the game, Greg came walking through the Breslin Center tunnel entrance after driving 90 miles per hour (by his own estimate) from the Detroit airport.

"Nice you could make it," the students in the crowd teased him behind our broadcast location. But he made it and he got paid for two games that day and he did again earlier this season without a hitch. When broadcasting games is your livelihood, you do as many as you can.

SEAN MCDONOUGH Network sports stars can live somewhat in obscurity from their brethren of yesteryear. When I grew up, with no cable television, there were very few network games as compared with today. Therefore there were few network sports announcers, so those in the business were well known to the public.

Sean McDonough is one of the lead announcers for CBS Sports, yet not many people probably would recognize him walking the streets of America. I met him this past spring—he is a friend of Michigan State assistant basketball coach Tom Crean and I was invited to fill out a foursome on the golf course when Sean visited here.

Here's a guy who did the play-by-play for the World Series for CBS in 1992 and 1993. He did the play-by-play of the Olympic hockey coverage from Nagano, Japan, back in February. He is a lead play-by-play man for the NCAA basketball tournament. He calls the shots from the 16th hole tower at the Masters; He does the play-by-play of college football and the college World Series among other assignments—but with so many network announcers anymore his name does not bring instant recognition.

I enjoyed visiting with him. He's from Boston and also calls the Red Sox games for the local television stations in New England. Baseball is his first love. I told him what I admired most about his work was his versatility—he is equally proficient at calling Olympic hockey as he is with golf. It's quite a trait that few in the business have.

WALTER ADAMS   He is not seen as frequently around Michigan State anymore, but Walter Adams is as close a figure to "Mr. MSU" as there is. He is still a fixture at home football games, standing under the goal posts, congratulating all the players when they leave the field, win or lose. But as I write this he is ailing and I am worried about him.

Walter loved college sports and he loved to heckle opposing coaches in baseball and basketball in his heyday. But time changes everyone's outlook on life and Walter eventually went from heckling Bobby Knight to becoming a close friend.

Every time the Indiana basketball team visits East Lansing, Walter stops by the morning shootaround to say hello to Knight. They've even had dinner the night before games. It is well-known that Adams presents Knight with some sort of gift just prior to the tip off of the game that evening and Knight plays along with the routine, occasionally giving Walter a gift in return.

Walter is a veteran of D-Day and he gave me one of the nicest gifts I have ever received. He made the pilgrimmage back to Normandy in 1993, one year before the 50th anniversary of the famed Allied invasion. He didn't want to get caught in all the hoopla and the crowds.

Walter knew that I am an avid World War II buff and upon his return, he called me to his office on the MSU campus. He had visited all five of the invasion beaches and brought home some sand from each. He placed the sand in small test tubes and labeled each with the date and the specific beach from which it was gathered. He put a test tube from each beach in a cigar box and gave it to me. I was very touched to say the least.

One of the tubes broke a short time later and Walter managed to replace it for me. I loved visiting with him about his involvement in the war. His eyes welled up recalling some of his fallen comrades. I told him it bothers me today that young people don't really appreciate the incredible sacrifices America's seniors made in their youth to preserve the country's future.

Walter taught economics and he was quoted often. He was considered an expert in his field and he also served a short time as interim president at MSU. He did not seek the job full time—he loved teaching instead. His name will always be associated with the noteworthy people who helped Michigan State University grow and develop.

BILL RUSSELL I met the former NBA great one time—he accepted an invitation to be a guest at Earvin Johnson's golf outing several years ago at Walnut Hills Country Club. Such occasions are a gold mine for television stations—plenty of celebrity interviews are readily available at a time of year when not much locally is happening.

Russell stood in the lunch line minding his own business talking to no one in particular. He finally was recognized and wanted no part of doing any interview. He also refused to sign autographs that day for the kids in attendance—and the Lansing youth programs were the beneficiaries of the event.

I asked the tournament organizers later, "If he didn't want to talk to anyone, why did he bother to show up?" This was a day of fun at a golf outing and Russell was in no mood for charm. I never did find out how he treated his golf partners that day. He was never invited back.

MUHAMMAD ALI In 1993, Muhammad Ali was invited to "speak" at a dinner in Lansing at the Radisson Hotel and I was asked to emcee the event. This was a boxing benefit—and I have never thought much of this sport. In today's world, teaching kids to beat up each other, even under supervision, seems out of date. But my friend Bob Every asked me to do it and so I agreed. I always felt bad for Bob because he was dedicated to a couple of local fighters who were on the brink of making some money as professionals—Roger Turner and Joe Lipsey. Problems in their relationship developed as the pro side of their careers developed and Bob was left with little more than some frustrated and bitter feelings.

He revered Ali, as many do and bringing him to Lansing was a big deal. Several hundred attended and I was stunned at how the champ struggled physically just to make it to the head table. His speech was restricted, but he managed to tease the waitress about the options he had for dinner. He picked at some chicken and while we sat next to each other, we didn't spend dinner chatting away. His mind seemed sharp and he was in a good mood, but the rigors of boxing had taken their toll. Instead of making a speech, he offered a few words and then performed some magic tricks. The crowd was thrilled at anything he did. The flash bulbs popped often that night—people swarmed to get their picture taken with him after the program. I think Bob Every enjoyed the whole thing as much as anyone.

BOB GROSS I've had very few athletic triumphs in my life, but on April 20, 1967, I began my senior baseball season at East Lansing High School by pitching a no-hitter. That limited achievement was chronicled in the State Journal the next day by a young writer named Bob Gross who had joined the paper only a short time earlier. Of course I still have the clip to this day—and that story was one of thousands Bob Gross would write about high school sports until his untimely death in June of 1995.

Bob and I became friends soon after I joined WJIM-TV in 1971. He had been in the media in this area longer than I had and I always respected his work ethic. He absolutely loved covering the high school games and knew all the area coaches like they were his own family.

I could rarely get any kind of significant high school "scoop" because all the coaches gave them to Bob out of their respect for him. He loved covering the smaller schools and he gradually took total charge of the newspaper's prep coverage.

He fielded many complaint calls over the years—readers are only interested in their particular teams and athletes—and for the most part he handled them all with dignity. I never knew how he could deal with the constant daily stream of gripes that he would answer calmly on the telephone.

Often times I would need high school scores not reported to our station and a call to Bob would always take care of the problem. I always appreciated his friendliness and his loyalty to me personally.

I was embarrassed to speak at a high school gathering one night where Bob was omitted from the program. The occasion was Paul Cook's retirement dinner when he stepped down as basketball coach at Lansing Eastern High School. It was a big deal with several hundred people in attendance. About ten people were invited to speak and I was one of them. Jud Heathcote was also on the program.

The night of the dinner, I noticed in the program that Bob Gross was not among the speakers. I couldn't believe it. He had more of a relationship with Cook than any other media member anywhere. I watched Bob sit in the audience that night wondering what he must have been thinking as speaker after speaker who had far less involvement with Cook would offer their praises.

The next day I called him.

"If I had known in advance that you weren't one of the speakers," I told him, "I would not have spoken myself. You should have been the keynote speaker!"

He was disappointed that the committee hadn't asked him to become more involved, but he was gracious about it and he thanked me for the call.

When Michigan State won the NCAA basketball championship in 1979, Bob joined me and Duane Vernon to hastily assemble a victory parade down Michigan Avenue to the State Capitol. We only had a couple of days to put the entire scenario together and as you know, Duane Vernon has gone on to become adept at organizing parades!

Bob invited everyone to a conference room at the State Journal and the other necessary officials from police, fire and the mayor's office were all in attendance. That parade to this day probably drew more people than any other in the town's history. Bob and Duane and I walked the entire route from the Frandor Shopping Center to the Capitol and we were all very proud of how it turned out.

When Bob Gross put his hand to such projects, they were always successful. He was an integral part of the Diamond Classic

High School baseball tournament. While he was not the event's director, he was a part of the committee and his efforts helped it grow substantially over the years.

Whatever high school sports have become in mid-Michigan, I steadfastly believe Bob Gross did more to foster their growth than any other individual—bar none. I miss the various events we both would sometimes attend. We'd go stand in a corner of various press boxes and solve all the problems of the world. I always hear people remember those who have passed on by saying "he'll be missed." In Bob Gross's case that is certainly more than a catch phrase.

DUANE VERNON Having mentioned Bob Gross, a few words about Duane seem appropriate since he is a valued member of the community in many ways also.

Duane is one of those guys everyone likes because he is genuinely friendly. He loves Michigan State and those who have seen his basement plastered in green and white know what I mean. It is almost like a museum.

He is the founder of the Michigan Parades Into The 21st Century, which has become a regular event in town each May.

People who know him ached for him when his first wife passed away after a difficult battle with cancer. He was very brave and upbeat through it all and he is remarried to a wonderful person who keeps him looking younger than his years.

Duane looks at life from a positive angle. For all the controversies that tend to surround college athletics and have certainly plagued Michigan State, he always finds a silver lining.

Like myself, he at one time harbored interest in the athletic director job. I told him he would have been great except for all the hassles that go with it. The coaches liked him and he would have worked well with them. He has been very successful running the Greater Lansing Credit Bureau. He is a loyal Spartan no matter what the won-lost records are.

He hosts a Super Bowl party at his Lansing home each January and the thing has grown to where you can barely get inside his house. Many of his other friends help him with extra television sets and bar tending, but it is pretty much a Duane Vernon Production. I've always told him if you want to visit with friends you don't always see, that's the occasion to do it—but you may not always see the plays of the game.

It was at one of Duane's Super Bowl parties where I spoke for the final time with the great Lansing human relations advocate, Dick Letts. His cancer was in its infancy and we spent nearly an hour reminiscing. That conversation is my most memorable moment from a Duane Vernon Super Bowl party.

DICK LETTS From Bob Gross to Duane Vernon to Dick Letts. Three guys who have offered enormous contributions to the community and like Gross, Letts is now gone. I'd known him for years and I've always said that one reason Lansing seems to have fewer racial problems than other cities is because of the work of Dick Letts.

He had a smile and a friendly word for everyone and he always liked to brag to me that he could beat me on the golf course "by just using my trusty five iron."

Letts, like Vernon, was a loyal Spartan. He was called in to solve many human relations problems and somehow he got both black and white people to listen to his reason. He always preached against violence but he could be tough when he had to be.

He knew many people and he was respected by just about anyone who ever met him. He chose to stay in the background with some of his roles, but I always believed he would have been a fabulous politician because he was so fair and so likeable. I don't see how the community can ever find someone who can achieve the racial solutions he offered.

DR. ROY SCHROEDER I met Roy in the summer of 1975. He was the pastor at Ascension Lutheran Church in East Lansing. He retired from his active ministry on August 31, 1996, and it was my high honor to be asked by our congregation to emcee his retirement dinner and program.

He became more than just a minister over the years. I am the first to admit that I have had few major crises in my life. But when troubles did crop up, Roy Schroeder helped me in more ways than he'll ever know.

A minister's life is not always easy and there were times when the roles were reversed. We'd go to lunch and just like a sports show, I'd give him my two-cent opinion. Everyone needs someone to talk to, someone you can trust and perhaps someone away from your family. In my case that someone was Roy Schroeder. For a period of two years during the early 1980s I found myself in his office on a weekly basis, drinking coffee and listening to his reason.

He is a brilliant preacher, at least in my own, biased opinion. I have copied in my own walk of life some of the techniques he has used on Sunday mornings. His son Paul is a good friend who has accompanied me on several basketball trips when I announce games.

Roy married off my brother and sister-in-law and he okayed my children to take communion in my church even though they attend a Catholic church and school at the same time.

My good fortune occurred when I met Roy 23 years ago.

CHAPTER 11

Parents

My wife and I had our three kids a bit later in our lives—when Tom was born, our first, I was 38 years old. Anyone who has ever been a parent knows one thing for sure—it is an inexact science that is based on experience and instinct. Parenting requires a tremendous commitment to the welfare of children. It requires many different skills and none of us probably have a command of them all.

I tell my wife I got a bonus in parenting simply by observing the mothers and fathers of thousands of athletes over the years. I studied the kids they developed and the methods they used. My observations have framed my own parenting game plan.

Obviously, times change. When I grew up in the 1950s and 1960s, we didn't have the incredible technology of many products now available today. I never felt my brother and my sister and myself ever wanted for anything. We were blessed. We came from two dedicated parents with values. Our best interests were vital to them both. Both were and still are quite conservative. I was raised in an autocratic household. I knew no alternative lifestyle. I didn't know much about segregation. I lived in a community with no minorities. There were probably three minority kids in my high school senior class of over 300. I knew nothing about poverty. I was spanked but never abused. My parents were interested in the various sports my brother and I played. My sister didn't play on high school teams because there were none in those days. And she didn't end up being a cheerleader either.

I'm the first to admit that my kids are spoiled and so are most of the kids they know. They play on many organized teams in a variety of sports—soccer (outdoor and indoor), hockey, basketball, football and baseball, not to mention lessons in tennis, golf, skiing, and swimming.

They don't relate to me when I tell them that when I grew up I played on one organized baseball team in the summer and that was it. The rest of the time my friends organized the various games at the nearby vacant lot. We made our own rules, devised our own leagues, served as our own officials. And we had a ball. We depended on each other.

The facilities available in mid-Michigan today are incredible. Huge basketball arenas with many courts have been built, complete with scoreboards, bleachers and concession stands. Ice arenas are indoors. When we played hockey it was always outdoors and there were no sideboards or goals. We used snow piled up along the sides of the ice and firewood outlined the goal areas. We had fun, too.

We never enjoyed indoor tennis courts, let alone adjoining exercise rooms. When we grew up we thought what we had was fully state of the art and modern—and, of course, then it was.

When I watched televised sports, I was happy to watch the "Big Ten Basketball Game of the Week." Bill Flemming was the announcer and he didn't have an analyst. Today virtually every league game is televised somewhere. There were six bowl games—today there are six million. When I watched the NHL, there were six teams—today there are six million. Major League baseball had two eight team leagues—today I don't really know how many there are.

There was no ESPN, let alone cable television. We didn't even have that in the first nine years I anchored television sports! My son prepares himself for school each morning watching ESPN's Sportscenter. No wonder people think he knows more about these players and teams than I do.

And no wonder my own parents look at what my kids have today and shake their heads. Times change and obviously so does parenting.

Money, of course, is one constant in our world. The problems are vastly different for kids who come from homes with money and those who have very little. That was the case when I grew up too.

I told my three sons: "Don't look for me to go to your coaches and campaign to get you more playing time. I've watched too many parents make life miserable for those who coach their kids."

My oldest is not a starter in basketball and he rides the bench a lot. He tried out for a team though he knew he might not play all the time. It's the chance he took. Of course, I hope he gets to play because he is disappointed when he has to watch like any other substitute. But I will not confront his coach about it.

I don't believe fourth graders ought to be playing on highly competitive teams, but I won't complain to the coaches about that either. To me, participation and fun should be the only reason for young kids getting involved in sports, but I don't see some parents agreeing with me in that regard. They want their kids to play to win and it is my observation that many parents use their kids' sports as an extension of their own lives.

I have nothing against competing and playing to win. It is an essential ingredient in what has led America to be a world leader. But to me sports should be an outlet for no-pressure fun, especially for youngsters.

I tell my own kids—play for the fun of it, period.

The best sport my oldest has been involved with, in my view anyway, has been tackle football. He wanted to do it—I didn't push him. It has taught him discipline and the true meaning of teamwork. He has learned what it means to sacrifice for the good of the team. He has enjoyed it, but it is a far bigger commitment than he has had to make in any other sport.

I wasn't big enough to play competitive football, but I have always appreciated its difficulty. I have never been a fan of soccer—to me that was a sport we played in physical education classes to just run around and release some tension during the school day. For those who love it and whose kids play it, fine. I think it is way overrated in terms of young kids learning much of anything, though. My wife disagrees with me and she is an educator. But I stand my ground with her on soccer!

Parents have kids involved in so many different sports today and that has both good and bad consequences. On the one hand, kids get to sample many different physical activities and they can then veer off into those they enjoy the most and play the best. On the other hand, many American kids, by not concentrating in one or two sports, probably do not become very proficient at them either. This is a tough call for both kids and parents. At a young age, I have always recommended participation in many activities pressure-free from parents' prejudice. My kids all play soccer even though I am not a fan of the game.

Clearly, parents have to set a good example at these games. Not just for their own kids, but others on the court or on the field.

I have witnessed parental interference on my own kids' baseball team. Fathers would shout instructions to the kids during games, directly counter to what the coaches' instructions were. I saw one coach get so mad he gathered all his second graders around after one game and told them he was quitting right then and there. I had trouble explaining that one to my son later that night.

My oldest plays on an all-white basketball team. One afternoon last winter his team played an all black team. It was a well played game with good sportsmanship and it was very close. Before it was over, a white official had to eject a black parent from the gym and it turned into a racial situation. It did not end then and there either—the two of them were going jaw to jaw in front of all the players immediately after the game ended. I also had trouble explaining that one later that night. What a scene for those kids to witness after they played with sportsmanship.

Parents' behavior at some of these games, from little league to the high schools, is an utter disgrace. Poor parental behavior in the stands is not even a rare occurrence. I see it at virtually every game I attend, whether I am covering it for my job or attending as a parent.

Charles Barkley likes to say that kids learn racism from their parents and I agree. Kids are taught about those of us who are black and white and Hispanic and other minorities and they form their attitudes from there. My youngest asked me recently, "Dad, is Michael Jordan black?" After I got done chuckling I realized he was serious about the question. How I answered him could have a profound effect on what attitudes he forms from that point onward.

I can't tell you how many times over the years I've had parents call me and nominate their own kids for "athlete of the week" or suggest we give coverage to someone "because they deserve it and they work hard."

I've had parents send me stat sheets on their kids. I've had them call me to report that their son or daughter just broke 80 in a

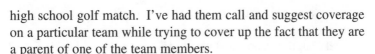

high school golf match. I've had them call and suggest coverage on a particular team while trying to cover up the fact that they are a parent of one of the team members.

When I cover high school sports, dealing with the parents is far more difficult than dealing with the coaches or the players. Parents think they understand how local television news works in terms of covering stories. Most of them do not and when they call to complain they do not want reality explained to them—so usually I do not argue with them for very long. I can only imagine how frustrating it must be for newspapers who cover all of the area high schools on a regular basis.

Very rarely have I ever had a parent write me a note, let alone call me and thank us for covering their son or daughter. I can't even remember the last time it happened. They will call and ask us for a tape of the show—we get that request all of the time. But never can I remember a parent adding "and by the way it was very nice of you to feature that story on our son—I just want you to know he appreciated and so did we." Dream on, Tim!

Not that we choose stories expecting to get showered with praise for our kindness and generosity—of course that's not what the game is all about. But dealing with stubborn parents is not an enjoyable part of covering sports.

I've seen what difficult parents can do to high school coaches. George Fox could probably still coach as well today as he could at Lansing Everett High School back in the 1970s when Earvin Johnson was around. But he got tired of all the hassles of the administration and parents and quit after the 1980 season. He really doesn't miss it either. Doug Herner left prematurely at Sexton. Stan Stolz had a long run at Okemos in a prominent school district—he retired while he still had his peace of mind. He has often told me, "I don't miss the parents."

In that regard it's amazing to me that guys like Paul Cook and Jeff Smith have hung around for so long. Paul is retired from being a teacher. He still loves coaching basketball so he agreed to take the girls varsity teams at Lansing Catholic Central High School.

"I go year to year," he says. "I stay with it as long as it's fun and as long as my health holds out."

Paul has coached in parochial and private school, boys and girls. He's seen and heard it all. Because he has 14 kids of his own, he knows all of the travails of dealing with young people and their parents.

Jeff Smith has coached varsity football at East Lansing for 27 years. He has had enormous success and he has coached through wide changes in that school system's administrative people.

"I've stayed with it because I've been able to keep most of my assistants with me," he told me. "I like working with the kids and I have been able to deal with most of the parents. I don't mind it when a parent asks me about his son's playing time."

The greatest tribute I ever saw given to a high school coach was given to Smith in September of 1997. He obviously had left a lasting impact on his former players.

A number of them met and decided to honor him at a special dinner. The program would also include Smith's long-time assistant coach Jack Piotter. The parents of the former players had nothing to do with this plan—this was the players' salute. I was asked to emcee the event months in advance.

The program was incredible. More than 200 players assembled from all over the country. They produced a video and offered testimonials, many of them humorous, to Smith and Piotter. They gave them gifts and posed for numerous pictures. They had the current East Lansing High School team and band on hand for a portion of the evening. Smith and Piotter were picked up and dropped off in a limousine.

In my remarks I told the group that most times coaches only get thanked when they retire. These guys took it upon themselves to say thank you while the coaches were still active. The entire event moved me a great deal. Maybe Smith and Piotter figured out a way over all the years to deal with all those parents and administrators to make the experience for the players a happy one.

In fairness, there are many good parents too. They get involved in the booster clubs and they support the coaches. They stay away from the issue of who plays and who is a substitute. They support their kids in all of their pursuits and they just don't tell their kids what they want to hear. They offer their love but they offer some frank objectivity too.

I wish parents would appreciate the values their kids get from good coaches who are also good people. If you trust your son or daughter around a coach, don't interfere. Let them bond with their coaches on their own. And parents, in my judgment, do not have the right to make a coach's life miserable just because their own son or daughter is not a starter. That's not fair to the other members of the team, let alone their parents. They have the right to have their own kids work with coaches who are free from the harassment of other unhappy parents. These coaches do not get paid enough to put up with some of this grief.

When I watch my own sons play, I find it a natural instinct to want to yell out instructions to them either on the field or on the floor. There can be nothing wrong to offering your kids and their teammates encouragement. I'm learning, however, that I must be sure to draw the line so as not to interfere with the instructions of their coaches. There's enough confusion in these games as it is without kids trying to figure who is right—the coach or mom and dad.

CHAPTER 12

News You Can Use

My major in college was not television or radio—hold the laughter, you've figured that out, right? I was a journalism major at Michigan State, Class of 1971. I completed my undergraduate degree in four years, plus two summer terms. I worked almost a full load at various newspapers and broadcast stations through it all. I had the maximum number of credits in journalism an underclassman could take. My cumulative grade point average was 2.8 on the 4.0 scale. I wasn't all that interested in the core courses, but I did very well in my area of interest, journalism.

I grew up thinking I'd be some kind of a sportswriter. I envied those in the business who got to cover all the big games and write their opinions in columns. I enjoyed writing and was dead serious about becoming competent at it. That's one reason I agreed to write this book and for no profit either. I wanted to experience the thrill of authoring a book for the first time.

Midway through my college years, a local radio executive named Fran Martin asked me if I wanted to host a daily radio sports show for a few dollars. I had not done any broadcasting, but the idea appealed to me. He'd read my work in a local weekly newspaper and figured maybe I could do something similar on his station.

Simple as that, I now was a broadcaster. Through that job I met the man who was the television sportscaster at WJIM-TV, Channel 6. His name was Tom Larsen and he went on to work in Boston. I told Tom I eventually wanted to do what he did. One day he called and told me there was a radio news opening at WJIM and that I should apply because it would help me get my foot in the door at a bigger station. I landed the job, a part-time night shift anchoring local radio news. I did a bit of radio sports, but not much. Through this experience I learned what good and bad writing was all about in broadcasting.

I have never completely lost my interest in anchoring news shows. On a couple of occasions I was even approached about switching to news and I considered it. There were two problems—one, I had made my reputation in sports and I wasn't sure that would transfer in the public's mind. Secondly, my chances at outside income were far greater in sports. News people pretty much have to stick to their main reporting job and that's it.

Over the years, my bosses took notice of my writing and in that regard, I now tell you about one of my favorite people I have worked for, Paul Brissette.

He is a North Carolinian who owned a group of middle-sized stations around the United States in the 1980s, including WILX-TV in Lansing. He is very bright and good with people. He took a sincere interest in my family for which I was always appreciative. He was in his early 60's in 1995, when he sold WILX-TV and the rest of his stations. Paul would often fly around the country in his corporate jet to visit his properties so I saw him often. He was a big sports fan and we enjoyed that kind of conversation on a regular basis.

In 1993, WILX-TV became unionized after a difficult 18-month period of negotiations. A strike was narrowly averted and in the final hours before a walkout, Paul was able to complete a labor agreement. He was in the process of changing some personnel when he took me to dinner one night in Jackson.

"Would you be interested in a dual role of sports anchor-news director?" he asked me. I had been tipped off by other management people several weeks previous to our meeting that he was going to approach me about the subject, so I'd had time to think about it and prepare a response.

I was interested and I wrote a plan for him about what I would do with such a job. He bought into my theories that night and we struck a deal on a napkin, much the way Bo Schembechler did when he was negotiating a Tigers' contract with Tom Monaghan.

I was mainly interested because I have vastly different opinions about the way local television news is aired than what has been standard practice.

I told Paul I would try to strengthen staff morale. No television station has everyone happy at the same time for a variety of reasons. What is important is to get everyone as content as possible. I was determined to make everyone feel a part of the team and I wanted suggestions as to how we could improve. I've always felt that good ideas are buried in the minds of workers in many companies never to be unearthed because their job titles just aren't significant enough.

We were not the number one station in the news ratings for a variety of reasons and I made him no promises in that regard. I told him I wanted to change the basic news content away from frivolous violence that had little impact on the vast majority of the viewing audience.

I promoted a number of other people on the staff to do most of the daily legwork for me and I basically oversaw the operation. For anyone considering a dual job like this in the future—forget it. It simply cannot be done without one of the jobs suffering.

Brissette was also in the process of changing the station's general manager and he asked if I had anyone in mind. I suggested our competition's top guy, Grant Santimore, a friend of mine but someone whom I had never worked under at any station. I was surprised that Grant was interested, but over the next several months Santimore and Brissette worked out a deal for him to leave WLNS-TV and take over at WILX. In my judgment, Channel 10 began to make a seriously competitive move in the market with that hire. Shortly after Grant took over in June of 1993, we promoted Cherie Grzech from assistant to head news director. This was initially my idea because Cherie was being offered jobs in other markets and I felt we should keep her. I knew I could not continue the grind of two jobs. If I did, the quality of either would not live up to my standards. Grant agreed to the move and I took a new title as Vice President of News and Sports. Besides my sports work, I basically helped advise Grant on a daily basis about station matters.

My involvement in this end of station work was demanding and sometimes frustrating, but Brissette was a terrific owner. He and Grant became close friends. A short time into his general managership, Grant underwent surgery at the Mayo Clinic to have a brain tumor removed. He missed very little work, which impressed me greatly and Brissette never once considered removing him or altering his job assignments because of his health problems. I learned a great deal from both men in the time I worked with them.

Fates are funny. When Benedek Broadcasting purchased WILX-TV in 1995, Santimore and Brissette were negotiating to purchase Lansing's ABC affiliate, WLAJ-TV. The plan was for me to move with them and host a half hour nightly sports show. We had many of the details privately mapped out. That ownership deal eventually did not materialize, however, and maybe it was all for the best. I now have 18 full years of service at WILX and the present general manager, Chris Cornelius, is truly one of the brightest guys I have met at any level of broadcasting. If he stays at the station, look out Mid-Michigan. In one year, WILX made enormous strides under his guidance. He has great people skills and understands the contemporary part of the business as few others I have ever met do.

So what does all of this have to do with news you can use? If I owned a station, my first move would be to drastically reduce the roll of the dreaded consulting services. The great Walter Cronkite himself constantly bemoans what consultants have done to local television news over the years. These services are expensive, running into six figures annually, depending upon their involvement with their various clients.

When I was in administrative work, I dealt with them on a regular basis. My feeling was they basically tell general managers what they want to hear, because that's the key to getting clients. Many of their people are simply former television news reporters who have gotten out of that end of the business for one reason or another. Then they become consultants, as if they have answers that other veteran television people do not have. Most have little knowledge of various markets and let me tell you from experience, American television markets differ vastly. What plays in Des Moines does not necessarily play in Lansing!

I believe they are useful for a couple of purposes, however. They are efficient at doing research which can help stations determine why people watch what they do. They are also good at locating future employees because they know about virtually every person in local stations across the country. They can also help get a competing personality out of the market. You tell your consultant to find so and so at station X a job somewhere else in the country. If they can do it, then your competitor isn't quite as good.

Why do people watch local television news and which stations do they watch? If someone could answer those questions accurately they'd be alone with the knowledge.

I believe most people watch a station out of habit. WJIM-TV went on the air on Channel 6 in the early 1950s and was nearly the only commercial station available to area viewers. They habitually watched Channel 6. I was the lead sports anchor there from May 1971 to June 1980. The so-called ratings in that decade were far better than what the current owner has today. Part of that success was because WILX-TV was very young and had very few resources. There was no competition. Today the market is much more competitive with many more players. Also, when I was at Channel 6 there was no cable television. Then, viewers had only a couple of stations to pull down as options off their rabbit ears. Today nearly 100 channels are available to local viewers.

I am also convinced that people watch news, local or national, because they like the particular anchors or they don't watch because they dislike like them. It takes time for personalities to catch on in any market, especially if they come from another locale. Americans today have difficulty agreeing on anything, let alone who they like and don't like to watch on television. This is where consultant research can become helpful. These companies ask many local viewers who their favorites are and why. The results help determine who gets rehired and fired. The dismissals of several local anchors in recent years in large measure were due to research which showed them to not be popular enough with a large audience.

As much as I loved Walter Cronkite, he never anchored the CBS Evening News against the multitude of stations available on cable. If he had, his ratings would not nearly have been as good as they were. Cronkite was the best and is someone who has my deep admiration. But the problems of local TV stations airing a competitive newscast today are much different than those facing the CBS Evening News in the 1960s and '70s.

There is much more of a tabloid tone to all television news simply, in my judgment, because of cable competition. The news better be entertaining as well as informative, or enough people just might not watch so as to make the program profitable. The so-called sex scandal coverage regarding President Clinton early in

1998 was a classic example of what I'm talking about. This story led the network news coverage night after night, even when there was little substance on a daily basis. But it was a titillating story that the public was curious about. The networks served up plenty of tabloid-style coverage to keep viewers tuned in.

A question I am frequently asked is why sports get so little time during the newscast. It has varied over the years, but three-and-a-half minutes is the norm at six o'clock and four minutes is standard for most nights at 11, except on the weekends.

I am the first to admit that general sports news has limited audience appeal. Research shows that many people could care less about seeing the Pistons highlights on any night, or the Tigers, or any others for that matter. They can go to ESPN, or Fox, or CNN or any of the other similar cable half hour sports shows to get all the national highlights they like.

My argument for more sports time is that stations have rarely considered how sports popularity can grow when different human interest stories are aired. What would you rather watch—the latest drug killing downtown or a story about a kid who lost a leg in an accident, but through determination has still found a way to play on the high school golf team? I claim many human interest stories that are sports related go uncovered because there simply is not enough time during the regular sports segment to air them. Almost anyone, in my judgment, would be curious to see these types of human interest sports stories. And I enjoy airing them far more than showing the nightly menu of professional sports highlights.

How about weather? Research shows that weather interest among viewers is nearly 90 percent. I say baloney. Any thinking human being who watches television news wants to know what the forecast is going to be so as to make personal plans. So that figure to me should be closer to 100 percent. But do viewers want nuclear-powered weather? By this, I mean do stations get more viewers with more expensive weather equipment that looks gaudy but basically doesn't add a whole lot of substantial information?

You'd be amazed to know how much money stations spend on weather equipment trying to outdo their competition. And we all know how stations react when two inches of snow fall. The newscast is led with the weather forecaster predicting dire consequences tomorrow morning because of a huge storm moving in.

People go to bed restless with anticipation, but by the next morning miraculously it turned out to be a dusting, if that, and the day turns out to be just like any other normal day. I am not criticizing the weather casters themselves—they are doing what they are told to do and most are pretty good. Joe Kopecek is someone I always consult with about the weather before I make a basketball trip during the winter time. His accuracy is very good. But in my mind, complete accurate and useful weather information could be made on television newscasts in far less time than is currently provided.

What some of these stations do to attract viewers is enough to make someone like Edward R. Murrow turn over in his grave. How about the so-called lead anchor doing kitchen recipes during the early newscast? Usually it is a female, of course, and I feel this is an insult to the female viewer's intelligence. Instead of having this anchor spending her time in the field reporting a story of substance in the community, she's in the kitchen with some restaurant chef making healthy cookies. It's enough to make me want to change professions!

Are we suggesting that recipes will gather a woman's interest on the early news far more than a story with real meaning? You tell me.

Another pet peeve of mine is watching anchors who to me are more interested in "being on television" than being news reporters. I claim a number of news anchors I've known and watched over the years are frankly more talk show hosts than broadcast journalists. I think it's nice that many of them get involved in community events. This is encouraged by stations and consultants alike, but how many of them attend workshops periodically to improve their reporting skills?

The best pure journalistic anchor I've worked with in my tenure is WILX's Roger McCoy. He is a journalist who happens to anchor television news. He is a stickler for detail and he has a thirst for covering news stories anywhere in the world. He has a broad knowledge of many subjects and he works hard at being a good journalist—far more so than just being "good on TV."

The late Howard Lancour was also one of the best journalists I ever worked with. Howard was a superb interviewer and he also had many contacts in the community he had acquired over the years. He worked the telephones constantly and he had a keen sense of what made for an interesting story on the air. He got out in the community and covered many stories himself. You did not see him doing recipes in the kitchen with some chef!

The growth of cable television has made it more difficult to build a growing news audience, be it local or national. With so many channels, viewers have many more options today. Therefore identifying stories that large audiences want to watch becomes more difficult. This is where consulting firms become meddlesome.

I have difficulty often times watching lead stories on local newscasts and agreeing that the story choice should be at the top. Recently, one local station opened with a single-car fatal accident with a reporter live on the scene. Of course it is a tragedy and it greatly affects the lives of those who knew the deceased. But what about the enormous percentage of viewers who are totally unaffected by that choice of story. As they watch many might think, "If this is the lead story tonight, can there be anything all that important following it?" I suspect that many potential viewers then turn to something else figuring nothing else any bigger will be reported the rest of the newscast that will interest them. Of course stations must guess at a lead story each night, and on some days it can be much tougher to find a top story than others.

My dad, a superb marketing executive with Chevrolet, once told me that his company always wanted to be associated with whatever was "hot in the street" at any given time. I've never forgotten that phrase. Transferring the analogy, I always try to lead a sportscast with whatever I believe is "hot in the street". I believe newscasts should adopt the same theory. Among all the stories to be aired on any night, lead with whatever could be termed "hot in the street." If it isn't hot yet, then lead with what could eventually become "hot in the street."

Attracting a significant news audience is so difficult anymore, it always amazes me when I see some stations start up a newscast for the first time. No matter how much money they invest and no matter how good the quality, the program has a very slim chance of becoming competitive.

One local station began a newscast last fall and drew a four share in its initial ratings period. A share point is the percentage of homes watching television at the time tuned into a particular program. The spin from a station spokesman to the public was that "this is an astoundingly high figure." The reality was that this news program drew fewer viewers than the show it replaced. It also has virtually no chance for significant audience growth.

Even in a large market like Detroit, the new CBS affiliate has not begun a local news program. The management there realizes that to do so would require an investment of millions of dollars on a product that has little chance to become competitive.

Quality is also difficult to deliver. Even established stations, especially one in Lansing, is notorious for using anchor people with very little news experience. Over the years I've seen many so-called news anchors who simply were in the right place at the right time to land a good starting job. Their top attribute, however, was that they commanded a very low salary.

I should mention here that I was the beneficiary of such management wisdom. I got my start on television mainly due to the fact that I was a small investment risk. My first salary was $7,000 when I began at the old WJIM-TV back in May of 1971. The station did not have to invest a large sum of money on anchor talent because it practically had an audience monopoly. That was a great break for me.

But I should also mention that I have taken great pride over the years in working like a hungry dog looking for food. When I started, I worked 12 hour days—and that was the minimum! I wasn't married then, so I felt if I was going to keep the job I got lucky to land in the first place I would have to work like crazy to keep it.

I carefully studied veteran sportscasters and listened closely to others who had advice. I have long felt that many young people who get an early break in broadcasting today do not fully appreciate it. The first thing they want to know is how much they are going to get paid. When I started I would have worked for virtually nothing. Getting the opportunity was pay enough!

I see many in our business today suddenly ready to leave the building after an eight hour shift regardless of what else is going on. And if they can work less than eight hours that's an added bonus. I rarely see young people staying late in the building at night working on perfecting their craft. When I speak to students I always tell them the same advice I learned—there is no substitute for hard work. Those who are better prepared and who work hardest have the best chance at success.

Of course, there are things I wish I would have done a bit differently. When you're young you tend to think you know it all. I've said many things on the air I now wish I would not have said. I certainly could have listened better. My first boss, Harold Gross, used to tell me that I still had "some maturing to do." He was right but I didn't know it at the time.

If I've learned anything over all the years, it's to listen better, not talk more. People in television news need to listen more frequently to what those in the audience have to say about what they do and do not watch. I'm always trying to identify the news that people can use—it is a never-ending search. I've also learned that it is absolutely impossible to please every single viewer. I don't worry about that as much anymore.

The goal, as I see it, is to find out what stories will draw the maximum audience the maximum amount of the time. So far, no consultant, no station manager, no news director and certainly no sportscaster has ever been able to clearly identify the answer.

CHAPTER 13

Interviews

Over all these years I've come to one basic conclusion about reporting, print or broadcast—interviews can be very overrated when it comes to getting a truthful answer. I maintain that at least 90 percent of all interviews conducted in the American media today do not provide answers that the subject honestly believes. I believe most provide answers that the subject wants the public to hear and are not necessarily honest.

In sports, coaches and athletes, by and large, always seem concerned that any negative comments will come back to haunt them. No sport seems to have a monopoly on duplicitous answers—you can get the runaround from most anyone.

In sports, cliches are the norm—how many times have you heard these:

"We just have to play one game at a time."

"We have to keep our focus."

There are plenty more, of course. The best interviewers in the media can struggle to get an honest response if the subject is not willing to divulge true feelings. This problem is not confined to sports. How many politicians do you think really give a totally honest answer?

Creative sportscasting requires the judicious use of interviews—do they add anything to the show or are they boring with the same old answers we hear day after day? If the subject isn't honest can he or she at least be entertaining and/or funny? It's an endless struggle, believe me.

Most college and pro football teams have their coaches speak each Monday about the preceding game and the ones coming up during the season. Unless the coach happens to have a glib personality, not much of substance comes out of these sessions. If a coach is about to face a team that has a 0-5 record, this would be a welcome comment:

"Our opponent coming up is, frankly, a very weak team. We should beat this team handily. If we don't, we will have only ourselves to blame. There is no excuse in my judgment if we lose this game."

Many coaches might feel this way on the inside, but would never make such a statement. This is what they will say in front of the lights and cameras:

"I am very surprised this team is 0-5. They have some very fine players and they've just had some bad luck. They've had a couple of plays go against them that could have gone either way. I expect these guys to give us a very good game and we'll have to play very well to win. We are not taking them lightly. This should be a very tough game."

That's a standard reply. Very dull, very antiseptic—and who cares?

Coaches and athletes who comment on games they have just played tend to offer more insightful thoughts simply because the emotion of the moment tends to limit their time to come up with a political answer.

I say all this to tell you that it is rewarding to chase down interviews with people who are almost dead honest without regard to who gets upset with their comments. As I say, I estimate less than ten percent of all people interviewed today have this characteristic.

Jud Heathcote was always one of my favorites. He had two great qualities—he could be brutally honest and he was as entertaining as they come. My shows always were better when I had comments from Jud.

My highest admiration for Jud has nothing to do with basketball. It is his ability to instantly come up with entertaining comments on the spur of the moment. No one that I have ever met is any better at it. I once wrote a magazine story on Jud's one-liners and about his talent as a speaker. I pride myself on my own public speaking and have studied Jud very carefully. I have always been dead serious about trying to be entertaining and funny myself. It is a rare gift and Jud is in the minority.

During his 19 years as the Spartans' coach, Jud could not go to almost any gathering without being asked to address the audience. With little or no preparation he could entertain for hours. He knew plenty of off-color jokes, but he didn't need them to be funny. He had a tremendous recall of lines taken from earlier speakers during any particular event and he could jump on them with something that just hit him. He amazed me—the pressure on him to deliver at golf outings, alumni gatherings, et cetera, was immense. Jud never let them down.

Comments from Jud which made the air resulted in a couple of run-ins between us. We had very few over the years, but these two are memorable.

One Christmas break near his retirement I was in Florida and my assistant Matt Morrison was anchoring the sports. The Spartans were hosting their annual holiday tournament with an opening night luncheon preceding the games. All the coaches would speak to the MSU booster group and the media was always invited.

Jud would always go last because he was always worth waiting to hear. On this occasion, with microphones in front of him, Jud told some jokes to the audience of several hundred and they roared. Some of his comments were about the MSU administration and its problems with George Perles.

I had done a good job of selling my interview theories to Matt Morrison, who chose to air Jud's funny remarks instead of boring comments about how the tournament would go. When I returned home, Matt told me "we have a problem with Jud—he's mad at me for airing the jokes he told at the tournament luncheon."

Before I called Jud, I looked at the tape of the shows in question and absolutely fell over laughing. They were hysterical and perfect for the group assembled. But aired on television they offended some people and the criticism got back to Jud.

When I called him to smooth things over, he was hot.

"Don't you people use any better judgment than that?" he asked.

The matter was not resolved with this phone call so several days later I tried again from my home one morning.

"Look, Jud," I began. "If you want to get mad at someone, make it me. Matt just does what I tell him. He has to work with you on a regular basis and I'd rather you give him a break."

It got worse before Jud finally finished with: "I'm mad now, but I'll get over it." Eventually I guess he did.

Another time, Jud took his team on a two week Australian tour during the summer. When he returned I figured one of his coaches must have shot some videotape on a home camcorder. Indeed the coaches had and when I called they were more than happy to let me borrow their tapes so I could show some highlights of their trip on the air.

I had several hours of material to wade through and I figured I'd just pick out something from the Spartans visiting tourist attractions. Instead, I hit the jackpot.

One of the coaches taped Jud chewing out his team at halftime. Remember—this was a no-count exhibition game on a summer tour, but Jud was talking like it was the middle of the Big Ten season. I figured a clip of this would be far more entertaining. It took some careful editing for me to use it. I got a further break in that Jud was out of town for the first couple of days that I aired these tapes.

I used another clip of Jud getting a technical foul from a female referee. He was giving it to her pretty good and she didn't take any lip. It was great stuff and I laughed like crazy—until Jud got home and heard what I'd been doing every night.

His phone call to me went something like this:

"I've already chewed out my assistant coaches for giving you these tapes without my permission," he began. "Just what was your understanding about what you could and could not use?"

I did a little Texas two-step in my reply because I didn't want his coaches to get in any further trouble—after all, they were just helping me out. He eventually let this incident pass too.

Jud has helped me in many ways over the years, including his recommendation to the Big Ten that I join the league's basketball network to do play-by-play. I always appreciated it. He rarely criticized me for what I said on the air during the games except for one point.

"Why do you always have to mention my age?" he would ask. I'd try to tell him that many in the audience probably wondered how old he was—after all he was the oldest active Division I coach at the end of his career. That never seemed to satisfy him.

I always appreciated his honesty during interviews. He came as close as they come to telling it like it is... Jud and perhaps

Bobby Knight.

I spend a great deal of time cultivating a good relationship with Knight and I understand some of his frustration with the media. I wouldn't want to waste my time with inexperienced reporters asking naive questions either. Some coaches, of course, can deal with all the dumb questions better than Knight can. I always write and ask permission for an interview and I always send a thank-you note afterward. He always writes back.

Knight began at Indiana when I started on TV at WJIM back in 1971. He is a very thoughtful person and he will reward you with great stuff if you are prepared and know what subjects he enjoys addressing.

For all the boring interviews you fight to avoid every working day, comments from Knight are welcomed once a year when the Hoosiers visit East Lansing.

His most memorable moment in my experience occurred with one of my other reporters before a game in Jenison Fieldhouse back in the 1980s.

Fred Heumann worked with me then. He is now a fine sports reporter for WDIV-TV in Detroit. I sent him to the Hoosiers' game day shoot-around because I could not make it. He was edgy about trying to get an interview without an appointment, but at least he made the effort. It was his first encounter with Bobby Knight.

With the camera running, Knight stopped Fred after the first question.

"Stop the camera," Knight said. "Let's start this over again—just back it up and let's do it again from the top."

Knight went on to inform Fred why his question was dumb—he would suggest some questions and Fred could use them. No problem.

The camera never stopped rolling and when Fred repeated what Knight just told him word for word a smile crossed The General's face.

"Well, that was very good," he said in a totally condescending tone. "Now you've got it."

"You liked that question," Fred replied.

"It was great. You did a great job," Knight continued.

The interview went on another couple of answers and Fred staggered back to our studio.

"I've got very little for you," he informed me. "The whole thing was a disaster. He just made fun of my questions." Wrong.

I was stunned by what we had. An entire episode between Knight and a young reporter and it was absolutely hilarious. It went about two minutes and I told Fred this was the best stuff I'd ever seen. We would run it uncut and unedited.

After it aired, word got around that we had a noteworthy interview with Bobby Knight. Fred ended up selling it to several national media outlets including Home Box Office. What Fred Heumann thought at the time was a useless, non-informative, waste of time interview turned out to be one of the most entertaining pieces I've aired in nearly 30 years.

The ultimate comments to get from coaches and athletes is to record what they say behind closed doors in meetings and in the locker rooms. It is in those locations that their true feelings are expressed. Imagine having a microphone hidden inside the coaching rooms at Michigan and Michigan State the week of the big football game. You'd hear coaches discussing amongst themselves what they really think about the other team's strengths and weaknesses. You'd hear honest assessments of their own players and those of the other team. Such comments would provide legitimacy to interviews. But that's not the way it works. Interviews from the week of that game usually provide the same tired answers you hear year after year. Like I say, it is my experience that most sports interviews are overrated.

There are always exceptions of course. I remember back in the mid 1970s at the Big Ten preseason football meetings in Chicago an incident involving the legendary Ohio State coach Woody Hayes. He was sitting at tables with reporters including Bob Page, who used to work for me at WJIM-TV. Bob is now with Madison Square Garden as a studio host in New York.

Hayes was offering stale answers to benign questions when Page decided to ask him about his involvement regarding the NCAA investigation of Michigan State's football program. The blood rushed into Hayes' face and he slowly rose from the table to confront Page a bit more personally. The last I saw of them Hayes was chasing Page down the hallway of the hotel.

Equipment problems can add to the hassle. In 1972, Duffy Daugherty's Monday media luncheons were attended by only a handful of reporters. Today Nick Saban entertains an entire room full of people, many he doesn't even know.

In the 1970s we used film cameras. I was usually the only guy to interview Duffy on film. I would need enough comments from him to last for the week. We'd usually go several minutes and in those days you couldn't talk forever because once film was shot it could not be reused. Videotape today, of course, can be used over and over again.

After one Monday interview, my cameraman told me the film didn't go through the camera properly and not only did we not get the recording but he would need a few minutes to fix it. Duffy lost his patience and screamed, "Why doesn't that station buy you guys some decent equipment?" He left before we could do it over again.

Early videotape cameras were suspect too. I went to Joe Louis Arena in Detroit one day to cover both the Red Wings and a college hockey news conference. I'd made a huge investment in time but it would be worth it to land several good stories.

I always tell our camera people to check their equipment thoroughly before they leave on an assignment. When we arrived the record deck did not work properly. Our photographer asked other camera men to help him out since he was a new employee. An hour into the mission, we had parts laying all over the Joe Louis Arena floor. It took all the patience I could muster not to lose my temper completely driving 85 miles home with absolutely nothing to show for my day's effort.

Interviews can provide a tremendous high for me on the rare occasions that I think I've really landed something special. I always judge them by how I believe they will be received by the public. Too many times sportscasters air the same tired old comments from the same tired old sources. Like I say, if they are not totally honest then they have to be entertaining. Thanks to Jud and Bobby and the few others who have filled the bill over the years.

CHAPTER 14

Routine

I had been on television for 17 years when our first son, Thomas, was finally born. Cathy had suffered through two miscarriages and I was 38 years old when he finally came into the world. As any parent knows, a first child can turn a parent's routine upside down.

Our working schedules clashed. She taught school in the mornings and still does. I essentially worked afternoons and evenings then as I still do now. Our family life has always been fostered on the weekends for the most part.

I am frequently asked about what a typical day for me is like and the answer is that each day varies greatly.

When Tom was born I wasn't doing Staudt on Sports on radio. My mornings were free, so I stayed home. Diaper changing became a chore I gradually learned to tolerate. I was Mr. Mom and was pretty good at all the things mothers get charged with doing the most in raising infants. We did not use child care services per se, but we did have plenty of MSU students help us out as baby-sitters. At different times, students actually moved into a basement bedroom we fixed up in exchange for child care.

When Sue Prister of WVFN approached me about doing a radio talk show in January of 1993, my first concern was availability. How could I get to a studio for the noon hour when my wife would not yet be home to take over handling the kids? I asked if the show could be hosted out of my home and to my surprise she told me that would be no problem.

Some engineers placed what appeared to be a small television antenna on my roof and the sound was perfect—again to my surprise. I hosted the early shows from our master bedroom at my desk, all the while keeping an eye on my young boys. The bathroom was adjacent to the microphone and from time to time the sound of a flushing toilet could be heard a bit muffled over the air. Out of all the bathrooms in the house, the boys always chose that one.

I didn't mind the inconvenience at all. The show was growing and the routine seemed to work. After Cathy came home at 1:30, I was free to head to my office and begin my television day. Often times, I could do telephone work from my home in the mornings, including setting up stories and conferring with other staff. The great thing about the two jobs was that often times I'd be doing work that would benefit all my shows at the same time. When I'd line up a television interview, I'd make arrangements for the subject to also call in and be a guest on the radio.

Eventually the kids went to school and I moved the show into the radio station proper. This was a much better set-up for many reasons. I could get in early and go over each day's program in advance with my producer, Paul Nolan. He always had creative ideas and could enhance the program with his own production techniques.

I like to arrive at least 20 minutes before air time. Usually there are phone messages to return and commercials to revise. I used to air all the commercials "live," but found that without a break I could never catch my breath. Plus, it became a strain on my voice to talk non-stop for more than an hour. I do some commercials live, but most are pre-taped with enough audio effects to make them sound "live." They are frequently updated so that they do not become stagnant.

I generally prepare for each show with four newspapers handy—the two from Detroit, the Lansing State Journal, and USA Today. The Detroit papers are the ones I tend to use the most each day.

We have an open-ended policy on the radio. I go until I think it is time to pull the plug and rejoin the national network. This usually is between 1:15 and 1:30. The noon hour has worked well for me—people are heading to lunch and many are in their cars. Most radio stations put their heavy hitter programs on the air early in the morning and so the noon hour is free from much of that intense competition.

After the radio show, I leave the station and return home which is only ten minutes away. I'll go through the mail, grab something to eat and return calls on the voice machine. Usually by 2:45 p.m. I am at the WILX-TV studios; then I stay through the six o'clock news. I return home for dinner and am back at the studio by 8:45 to prepare for the late show. I am out the door of the studio the moment we sign off and walk in the house around 11:45 each night.

Cathy and I usually stay up another hour and rehash the day and watch television or read. Late night television is awful. I even have all the movie channels, but they don't entertain me much either. I'm usually asleep by 12:45 and then up in the morning when Cathy is getting the kids off to school at seven.

I try to stick to this routine and yet in the news business, change is a normal part of any week. I don't accept nearly as many speaking engagements as I used to make, mainly because the two hours at home in the evening is a chance to be with the family before the boys go to bed. When I do accept my wife sometimes goes with me, other times I speak between shows and hurry back to anchor the 11 o'clock sports.

I rarely have tired of all this over the years, and I have been very thankful for the opportunities I've had to do things I enjoy. Like anyone else, there are some days I am seething when I drive home at night, but not very many. I learned long ago that no matter how good or bad a day has been, it can all change for the better or worse tomorrow. I am always pleased to drive home having anchored what I believe are two good sportscasts—but I also realize that they mean next to nothing in terms of helping the next day's shows to be of the same quality.

For 13 years, from 1980-93, I commuted to the WILX studios in Jackson. There was always a business office in Lansing, but the anchoring and studio work was done out of Jackson. It was 33 miles for me door to door. Some nights I would actually drive home between shows for dinner, but it got to be a grind. In the warm weather, I'd meet the family in Mason and we'd eat outdoors.

Over those years I only received one speeding ticket and only had car trouble one time and that was in winter between the evening newscasts. A corrections officer from the Southern Michigan Prison in Jackson picked me up. I am grateful to him to this day.

Many times I should never have tried to drive home late at night because of the winter weather, but there was never much traffic so I always managed to make it. We had hotel privileges next to the station, but I never stayed overnight—that would just start the next day with a hassle trying to get home and go through the regular routine all over again.

In the 1980s, WILX did not have a microwave system, so the news tapes had to be driven from Lansing to Jackson before each show. We called this the "shuttle" and photographers would take turns handling that important chore. The entire news programs were contained within his mail bag and if for any reason he didn't make it, there would be no show. Often times, the drivers would wait until the last possible moment so as to include as much fresh news as possible. Consequently they would come flying into the parking lot and literally running into the building to hand the news tapes to the producer. This led to chaos on numerous occasions, not to mention a few speeding tickets along the way. But just like the mail service, our shuttle driver always made it, even if there were a few occasions when we actually had gone on the air for a few seconds before the news tapes arrived.

Eventually a microwave system was installed so that the tapes could be "fed" to Jackson and recorded for playback. It was an enormous improvement.

By the late 1980s, a new building was constructed on American Drive on the south side of Lansing. Eventually an addition allowed the station to finally be housed in one building. I felt like I had died and gone to heaven with the end of 33-mile one way drives. I was now a mere 15 minutes from the office by freeway.

When that change occurred, the perception of WILX as a "Jackson station" finally began to erode. The Lansing-Jackson market now had a full time NBC affiliate operating out of the state's capitol city. Since then, the competition for viewers has been on more level footing.

Many guys in my business like to get out in the field and cover stories away from the studio. I have done my share of that and still do, but it is not my preference. I now anchor two minutes in the 5 p.m. news, three-and-a-half in the 6 p.m. show and four minutes at 11 o'clock. This requires a great deal of in-house time which I enjoy.

I view a great deal of video tape which comes in both locally and nationally each day, trying to find the most entertaining "news." It is a challenge which I always enjoy. Hardly a day goes by in which there isn't an opportunity to give viewers a chance to laugh, separate from all the gore and violence they see during the early portion of the news.

In the 1970s and 1980s, much of local television sports coverage was devoted to "hard news." But studies have shown that for sports to fit within a local newscast there must be an appeal to those who are not hard core fans. I have always enjoyed chasing that segment of the audience. Today few viewers really care that the left tackle is injured and might not play in this Saturday's football game.

Bernie Smilovitz, the talented anchor at WDIV, the NBC station in Detroit, has always said, "For the couple of minutes you get each night, all you can do is try and entertain 'em."

He is absolutely right. When a sports story has significant importance it often times gets moved to the head of the newscast itself, such as when the Red Wings won the Stanley Cup. Some sports stories transcend the normal run of sports material and become "news" stories at the same time. When a team goes to the Super Bowl, often times the entire newscast will be aired from that site by stations whose entire staff is involved.

Hard-breaking sports stories still are of interest to a significant segment of the audience, but after that the day's highlights tend to get monotonous, night after night. Many stations do not even carry the regular season professional scores anymore and very few people have missed them.

With so little air time, there simply is no time to tell the few that are interested that "The Utah Jazz lead the Houston Rockets at halftime, 43-42."

Much of my nightly routine, therefore, boils down to finding the humorous and unusual moments from all the highlight clips. Airing those interests far more viewers than just the hardcore fans. I have found this to be true year after year.

When I started on television in the 1970s, sports was given five minutes per show. There was no cable television then so fans couldn't turn to ESPN to overdose on scores and highlights. In those days I aired much more national news because it was the only place that viewers could find the nightly results. With so many options today, the sportscaster in the local news has no chance to compete with the ESPNs of the world on a level playing field. So I maintain, to survive, you must be local and you must be entertaining. A shortage in either of those areas will not produce a program of significance, whether the journalism purists of the world like it or not.

Making news judgments is a tough call every day also. On December 30, 1997, I returned home from televising a basketball game at Purdue. At 2 a.m., I discovered on my voice mail a message from my substitute anchor. He told me he had run a story saying that Michigan State's Nick Saban was about to be named coach of the Indianapolis Colts, according to a report broadcast that night on the NBC station in Indianapolis.

This turned out to be completely erroneous, of course. Had I have been on the anchor desk that night, I likely would have made the same judgment call. Doesn't the NBC station in Indianapolis know what it's talking about in regard to the Colts? Why would it air such a story in a large and competitive market unless the story was absolutely true?

Sadly, some stations will air anything with little regard for accuracy. This story ended up getting national play, simply because everyone else figured the NBC station in Indianapolis had to have credibility in dealing with the NFL team in its own city.

I could find no fault with our people for continuing to follow that station's lead—even though the local media was also criticized for repeating merely what was being aired elsewhere.

Last spring, I was visiting with Nick in his office. We were talking about the constant NFL rumors and he said he really was telling everyone the truth—that he has no interest in being an NFL head coach—that he likes the set up he has at Michigan State better. But he added that he and his wife agree that such annual NFL rumors will likely dog him the rest of his coaching days.

CHAPTER 15

Radio

In 1969, I received a phone call out of the blue from an East Lansing radio station general manager named Fran Martin. I had never met him but he said he had learned marketing from speeches he'd heard my dad make over the years while he was teaching at Michigan State. Fran ran WSWM radio inside a big old white house located between Okemos and Williamston. That station today is WFMK. The music was easy listening and he wanted to add some local sports coverage. Fran had read my work in the East Lansing Towne Courier.

"Can you do radio?" he asked me.

Up to that point in my life, at age 20, I had given no thought to being a broadcaster. My future was in writing. I had never hosted any kind of broadcast show and never conducted an on-air interview.

"I'm looking for a five-minute, late afternoon radio sports show each week day," Fran told me. "You could drive out here after class and record it at your convenience."

The idea immediately intrigued me. The only schooling they'd give me was a short lesson on how to work a tape recorder. The pay wasn't bad either—$5 per day. Welcome to The Tim Staudt Show on WSWM Radio in the fall of 1969. No one ever told me whether my voice was good or bad. No one told me how to write radio copy. They just said do five minutes and leave room for a commercial.

It didn't take long for me to figure I could expand on this arrangement since I loved hosting my own radio sportscast. Soon I was helping Art Brandstatter, Jr., do play-by-play of the East

Lansing High School football games. Pretty hot stuff. The only thing they told me here was how to set up the equipment on location. I'd get there plenty early so I knew we'd make it on the air on time. Art would usually show up just before the opening kickoff. Sometimes I didn't hook the equipment up just right and that coupled with Art's late arrivals offered me my first doses of stress in the business.

Eventually I convinced Fran that we should broaden our horizons. Notre Dame was opening its new basketball arena and the first game would feature UCLA and its famed center Lew Alcindor (now known as Kareem Abdul Jabbar). There I was in South Bend, broadcasting that game to whoever might have been listening that night back in mid-Michigan.

After a couple of years of this, Tom Larsen, the WJIM-TV (channel 6) sportscaster, told me his station had an opening in radio news. I'd always told Tom I wanted to eventually work with him and then work my way into television.

It was in the spring of 1970 that I first met Tom Jones, the burly station manager at WJIM-TV and radio. He hired me after I met him at the Country House for an interview. I would do weeknight local radio news and some pretaped radio sports. Soon thereafter Tom hired another guy to take a radio shift—George Blaha.

By 1971, George and I hosted WJIM radio's play-by-play of MSU football. We did the famous 43-10 win at Purdue when Eric "The Flea" Allen ran for a new NCAA record of 350 yards. To this day that is still the greatest single performance I have ever seen by an MSU football player. To do it on the road made it even more special. George did more of the play-by-play than I did so my "color" consisted mostly of anecdotes and stats.

Once I became sports director of both WJIM-TV and radio, Blaha left the station and I did all the radio work. I did play-by-play of MSU football through 1978. In those days, any local station could air the games using its own announcers. About six of them did and those booths along the top deck of the press box at Spartan Stadium always featured the call letter banners of the various radio stations in town. We paid a rights fee of something like $500 per game. Today, of course, the Spartan radio network goes to numerous stations for nearly $500,000 a year in rights fees.

One year I called the games while the station's news personnel was on strike. The walkout affected the concession workers at the football game, some of whom would not cross a picket line set up around the stadium. I had to have police protection to get to and from the broadcast booth that day. Fortunately a settlement was reached shortly thereafter.

When Earvin Johnson arrived on the high school scene so did I to broadcast many of his games, which spanned three years. The most memorable was the regular season game against Lansing Eastern and Jay Vincent in Jenison Fieldhouse his senior year . The place was jam packed with 10,500 fans. Jay's team won 70-62, the only loss Earvin's senior year and the only time that Jay's team beat Earvin in his entire Everett career.

Early in my high school play-by-play days I learned some intangible hints. In Grand Rapids one night I broadcast a state tournament Regional game. The gym was packed and my location was in the middle of many fans. I literally could not get out of my seat from the time the game started until it ended. I knew I'd need some liquid to keep my voice fresh so I had about six cups of Coca-Cola handy. The problem arose after I'd drunk them all in the first half.

At halftime, let's just say I needed a T-O baby! I had no color man to help me and I knew the commercial breaks weren't long enough for me to go the restroom and return in time. It would be hard enough to get out through the crowd and return.

But when you gotta go, you gotta go. I said to heck with the broadcast quality, I'm out of here! We had about five minutes of halftime dead air that night. I wasn't proud of that moment but I sure was "relieved" when it ended. To this day I barely drink any liquids during games and when I do it is in small sips only!

Little did I know during the late 1970's that a weekly call in show, unusual at that time, would become a standard in the radio industry down the road. On Thursday nights, I hosted a call-in show and I can't even remember its name. We had a seven second tape delay then to prevent obscene language. It was an elaborate set-up. Today, listener comments that regularly make the air would have been zapped on that show. I had a friend sit in the studio with me and the two of us discussed the issues of the day.

In those days, I took all the various sports issues dead seriously and commented in the same way. Not as many people heard that show as listen to Staudt on Sports today and maybe it's just as well. I said some things I'm not very proud of in hindsight, but the show was well received and I enjoyed doing it. The problem was it backed up against the 11 p.m. TV news and so I would be running to get the late night TV sports finished before ten o'clock.

One of the main reasons I left WJIM-TV and radio in 1980 was to have the opportunity to expand my base. I made a specific salary at that station and had little chance to do outside work and increase my income. I had no contract—I worked strictly at the will of the station owner, Harold Gross.

I negotiated a deal with WILX that summer, which included the ability to pursue outside income. It led to some great opportunities, especially in radio. The salary WILX offered that year matched exactly what I was making at WJIM in 1980, but I would get a staff to help me and many other perks—including a non-exclusive clause allowing me to seek more programming than what was carried by my new station.

I immediately lined up some radio sports news reporting that did not entail much of my time and didn't make for much impact on the air. In the 1980's, sports talk radio around America was beginning to take off, but it really never entered my mind that this was an area where I could advance. I did not see how I would find the time and I didn't know if there was an area station with a format suited to this type of show.

In 1993, Sue Prister served as general manager for a group of area stations including WVFN AM 730 on the dial. The station had a good signal and carried all syndicated sports programs. Very little effort was put into making it a viable competitor in the market. We had been talking about my doing some other shows when she called me one day in Columbus, Ohio, where I was in a hotel room preparing for a Big Ten TV game that night.

"Would you be interested in hosting a half hour talk show?" she asked. We agreed to discuss it when I returned home the next day. I didn't know how I would be able to find the time. I was staying at home mornings with the three boys, none of whom were in elementary school yet. Cathy was teaching kindergarten in the mornings.

Sue wanted to call the show Staudt on Sports and air it at noon for a half hour. She said they could put an antenna on my home and I could do it from there. They would provide a producer. The offer was good enough that I decided to give it a go. Kyle Pierson was my producer, a very talented and dependable young guy.

Sue said we could start either in March or April. Even though I would be gone quite a bit on other assignments in March, I opted to start right away because delaying new programs leads to complications I didn't want to think about.

So on March 8, 1993, live from Okemos, in my bedroom, Staudt on Sports was born. I didn't know quite what to expect. The station had very few listeners. And I didn't know much about Kyle Pierson except that he was excited to be the producer and Sue Prister was anxious to get this show on the air.

Within three weeks, the advertising load expanded to the point where we increased the show to an hour. Staudt on Sports was growing daily. Everywhere I went people mentioned my radio show to me. We had very few technical problems although there were times when the sound of a flushing toilet would make the air. The bathroom was next to the microphone and the kids never had any second thoughts about coming in to listen and then using the facilities at the same time.

Like most broadcast properties, WVFN was eventually part of a mammoth station sale to Liggett Broadcasting. Staudt on Sports survived and I aborted several opportunities to move the program elsewhere. I wanted to keep my continuity at the same place on the dial at the same time slot.

By this time, I helped Kyle become employed full-time at WILX-TV and Paul Nolan became my producer and he has been with me since. He is very creative and we work well together. He knows high-tech radio equipment very well and his expertise in that area shows every day.

Our ratings have continued to grow and we dominate in men aged 18-54. Why have we succeeded? I've thought about this a great deal and the number one reason, in my opinion, is our attitude toward the show.

I simply do not take all these sports as seriously as I did when I was coming up the ladder. I have fun with the callers and I rarely argue with them. Even if I don't agree with them, I don't cut them off—I let them make their points so long as they are not offensive, slanderous or inaccurate about facts.

People ask me about memorable calls. One day a guy called who had just hit a deer with his car. His vehicle was disabled and he was waiting for the police to arrive. To while away the time he called Staudt on Sports.

Another guy told me of his lifelong love of the Detroit Lions. He was a regular caller. He told me he delayed his wedding a couple of hours on the spur of the moment because a Lions preseason game was on television. He wanted to see if rookie Jeff Komlo had any promise as a quarterback. He added that his wife was very upset about his decision that night.

We don't get many crank calls because we screen them all. I also subscribe to my dad's theory about concentrating each day on whatever is "hot in the street."

The day of or the day after big games, I don't want some guest on there spending 30 minutes talking about fishing. I don't want some author on pushing a book. I don't want some media guy telling the world all he knows when people aren't very familiar with him in the first place.

I do have some guests. My standard is that if I think they will add to the entertainment value of the show, I book them. Otherwise, this is a show for those of us who just like to sit around the table at lunch together and shoot the breeze about sports.

If a caller asks me something and I don't know the answer, I don't try to fool them. A simple "I don't know" works just fine. If I can find the answer for them, I try to do that.

I poke a great deal of fun at myself on the show. People don't like to tune in to another egomaniac radio host who thinks he knows everything when he really doesn't. That's not me. I just enjoy talking to the fans and having fun with them. I laugh a lot and as I say, I don't mind being teased. It's the old Duffy Daugherty trait: "Take everyone seriously but yourself."

When I began Staudt on Sports, I was very concerned about how much preparation the show would require. I don't have a lot of extra time in my day, but I want the program to grow, sound professional and offer something to all of the listeners on the noon hour. Because I work in the business of sports and television, my day is saturated with news already and so I perhaps don't need as much "study" time as other hosts do who do not have television commitments.

I let the callers dictate the subject matter—they don't have to apologize to me for bringing up a subject that seemingly has been beaten to death. If that's what they want to talk about, no problem with me.

I make sure that I focus on all of my advertisers. If you listen, you know that I voice most of the commercials, in the same
manner national newscaster Paul Harvey does. This works out
well for me in many ways, but I do not just accept any advertising. Clients must have a solid business reputation that I am familiar with, and I must use the product or service if I need it. I have
turned down some advertisers, believe it or not, even some who
were willing to spend big money with us. I will not compromise
what I believe to be proper standards for my recommending an
advertiser to the general public. I have had very few complaints
about my clients over the years. Most of them joined the show
simply by asking me how they could get on the program. Many
have been with me for most of the show's run and very few have
canceled. And it has been gratifying to receive mail and calls on
the air praising our clients.

I make a point to listen to other talk shows to educate myself,
and to see what works and doesn't work for other programs. My
biggest criticism is that too many hosts take all of this stuff way
too seriously. Sports at the talk show level is entertainment for the
most part. Sports do not matter to many people in this country, so
I'll bet America would survive if there were not college and pro
sports for people to praise and gripe about.

I'll listen to WJR's Sportsrap in Detroit as I drive home each
night for dinner, and I'm amazed at all the arguing I hear between
host and callers. It makes no sense to me and frankly it is uncomfortable listening. WJR attracts good guests but I believe the rapport with listeners gets strained—to the detriment of the show.

The hottest topics on Staudt on Sports are anything to do with
the Michigan vs. Michigan State rivalry. It is hotter among the
fans than it is among the schools themselves. Some of these fans
absolutely live and die with these teams. They don't look at the
other school as their "sister school" as former MSU football coach
Muddy Waters used to say. They're happy when their team wins,
and as long as the other team loses. The arguing between the fans
makes for entertaining listening and I do very little to stop it. In
fact, I bait some of these callers even more and I get a big kick out
of it. The week of the Michigan vs. Michigan State football game
is the week I enjoy Staudt on Sports the most.

Each day of that week I try to offer something unique regarding the upcoming game, including special guests. By Friday

we're at a fever pitch—the phone lines are tied up way before we ever go on the air. Paul Nolan adds music and special effects and everyone is ready to suit up and play themselves. To me, it's the highlight of sports talk radio.

Coaches hate these shows for the most part. MSU hockey coach Ron Mason thinks some of them go a long way in getting coaches fired. Waverly High School basketball coach Phil Odlum told me he doesn't like them because it gives uninformed fans a forum for which to vent their opinions. I think he has a point but I do not believe sports talk radio necessarily reflects the proportionate attitudes in the community about any particular topic.

When I hosted the show out of my home I wore a headset with two audio sources. In my left ear, my producer would tell me who the next caller was—"Jim from Holt is next, that's Jim from Holt," Kyle Pierson might say. In my right ear I would hear whatever was going over the air.

One day the show's subject matter was recruiting—always a fan favorite. The subject of Michigan State basketball recruiting was hot, and so were some of the fans who were commenting on Jud Heathcote's problems of luring better players to his program. I was dodging through the mine fields trying not to over- or under-state anything.

"Jud from East Lansing is up next," Kyle said in my ear. "That's Jud from East Lansing."

Gulp. Could this be the one and only? Why is he listening to this show?
Coaches never call in unless they are invited guests.

It was the one and only and he was in his car. He wasn't even the next caller—he had to wait for a couple of other guys to take some shots at him.

"You're always trashing us about our recruiting," he began. "Now let me set you straight on some of these players."

He proceeded to explain how several guys got away and the conversation ended up being reasonably cordial. Jud never hesitated to give me his opinion about the show.

I never know how a show is going to go when I walk into the studio each day. Paul and I just hope for the best. Of course, whenever there is a hot topic that has just broken on the local sports scene, we know we're going to have a fun time. We're unique—most shows have a specific time to them. I go from one hour to 90 minutes depending on the load of advertising and calls. An average show is 75 minutes and then we simply rejoin the One on One Sports Network. If you have never listened, give us a try. It is my goal to entertain you and make you laugh, and if I can do that then I feel like I have added something to your day. But don't ask me who the right guard is for the St. Louis Rams—I don't have a clue and I'd be worried about my sanity if I did know!

CHAPTER 16

Memorable Moments

When you spend 30 years in any one career, you work with many people who come and go and you are bound to witness a variety of incidents. Some of them are more memorable than others.

In the mid-1970s we had a weather man at WJIM-TV whose name was John. He also was a disc jockey on the radio station. He hung around at night to anchor the 11 p.m. weather cast on television. He was liked by everyone at the station and was very talented.

One night WJIM was to be honored at a dinner and one of the members of the anchor team was requested to attend to accept a plaque. We drew straws and John lost, so he had to go. It was one of those long cocktail dinners and it was in the summertime and hot. Dinner did not begin right away.

No one noticed when John returned to do his late weather show at around 10:30. The rest of us were busy preparing our own portions of the program. That was a mistake. John was very drunk. He tried to act like nothing was wrong, but once those hot television lights hit him in the studio it was like taking Mike Tyson's best punch.

Early in his forecast he fainted right on the air. He just disappeared from sight. His speech was a bit slurred to begin with and it wasn't until he began his weather cast that the director in the booth noticed that he was not acting normally.

He was laying on the floor out of camera range and they quickly cut to a commercial. Our news anchor at the time was a guy named Will Murphy. He decided to take over when they returned from the break.

"John received an emergency telephone call," he told the viewers. "So I'll finish the weather forecast."

Are you kidding me? That was the best plan, even on short notice?

Murphy did not even know what the forecast was so he just made it up. He was literally stepping over Sebastian who was still on the floor but out of camera range.

Naturally the phones lit up when the show ended. Viewers saw John go down and they knew his speech was not normal. Fortunately in those days, the shows were not normally recorded. If they had been, John might have been fired.

He was not the only one to draw the wrath of the station management. Those of us in the building that night also got tongue-lashed for not noticing his condition. John was suspended for a couple of weeks but he returned to the air.

The incident was the talk of the town for a while. The station employees laughed about it in hindsight. It was one of the funniest things I'd ever seen—but the station owner didn't find any humor in it at all. They tell me that one of our engineers actually did have a tape rolling that night and he had a copy of the incident. I never saw it and they kept the word quiet so as to protect John. I'd love to see it again today. I guarantee you no blooper on television was as funny as that one.

When I began at WJIM I had no assistants to help me, not even any interns. I was a one-man band. I never shot any film, but I wrote and edited all of my own copy. There was no weekend news in those days other than an 11 p.m. newscast on Saturday night. I had to anchor that program along with the shows during the normal work week.

When I did get some help in 1973, my first assistant was the former great MSU track star, Herb Washington. He went on to become a pinch runner for Charlie Finley and the Oakland A's, you may recall. Herb was a great guy, but he had absolutely no clue about television news. I sent him to the hospital one day to interview an athlete who'd just undergone knee surgery.

"Was the operation a success?" he asked.

The guy laying there moaned for a moment then responded, "I sure hope so."

Jack Russell was another assistant who was just getting started. Our management people did not like him on the air from the beginning and he didn't make very much money. We eventually added a full load of weekend newscasts and he anchored the sports. One Saturday night I was laying home in bed watching his late show before going to sleep. Jack was signing off.

"This will be my last night here on Channel 6," he said. "I'd like to thank [so and so and so and so] for making my days here very pleasant. I'd also like to thank the management of the station—but I can't." With that he was finished. He never called me in advance nor did he give anyone else forewarning.

My boss saw what I saw and immediately called me. He was livid. The next day I drove him to the airport and he was grumbling about it the entire ride. Jack was gone and I've never spoken to him since.

Bob Page, who is currently a successful sportscaster at the Madison Square Garden network in New York, worked for me when he was a Michigan State student. He had some classic run-ins with people because Bob was just naturally confrontational, even though he was a good guy.

One day he spoke with an MSU football player while hiding a microphone in his dorm room. Word of that got back to Head Coach Denny Stolz who was very upset to say the least. Another time he hid in the bathroom at a local high school trying to catch students using drugs. He also challenged Woody Hayes at the Big Ten football meetings in Chicago and Hayes chased him down a hallway. He was a classic.

Of all the games I've ever broadcast the most memorable was the 1974 Ohio State-Michigan State football game in East Lansing. This was on radio and Jim Hornberger was working the games with me in those days. The Buckeyes arrived as the number one team in the nation and they were well on their way to another victory, leading 13-3 in the second half.

Then Charlie Baggett passed to Mike Hurd for a touchdown and Levi Jackson made his famous 88-yard run. Suddenly it was 16-13 with less than four minutes to play.

The Buckeyes worked the ball down to the one yard line and as time was expiring Ohio State tried to run another play. There was total confusion. Hardly any players were set at the snap and Brian Baschnagel ran into the end zone with the ball. One official signaled touchdown and another signaled that time had expired.

This was in front of the tunnel entrance at Spartan Stadium and the officials immediately disappeared.

Thousands of fans poured onto the field and I could not say for sure who had actually won. Players on both teams were jumping up and down. Some guy stole the hat off Woody Hayes' head and he was in the middle of pandemonium looking for the referee.

Fans literally were leaving the stadium not knowing who had won the game. We stayed on the air. The Big Ten Commissioner, Wayne Duke, was in attendance and he went to the dressing rooms to get a definitive answer from the officials. But they had hurried out of the stadium back to the Kellogg Center where they were staying.

I sent Jim to the locker room to help us out and he raced out. There were still thousands of people on the field and I was describing everything I saw. Some 15 minutes later Jim ran back out on the field trying to signal me. He had a green blazer on and he took it off and pointed to it. I guessed that meant the Spartans had won and it was right. It was the strangest ending I had ever seen to any football game.

The teams opened the next season in East Lansing and the Buckeyes won a rock solid 21-0 victory. Hayes reportedly was in the process of aiding the NCAA in the investigation of the MSU program and he was still steamed over his team's loss in East Lansing the previous year. He also didn't like losing as many recruits in Ohio as he was to Stolz's assistant coaches.

The maddest I've seen any coach, surprisingly enough, was Tom Izzo. The MSU basketball coach is generally an easy-going guy and even when he is upset, he is under control.

But before his team's home finale in 1997 against Indiana, he lost it. I was walking through the hallway to the press room prior to the game. I was broadcasting that night with Greg Kelser. I saw Tom screaming at two MSU athletic department staffers. He was flushed with anger. Then he saw me and started screaming.

He was upset because there were several thousand Indiana fans in the Breslin Center that night and he thought it would erode his home court advantage. Maybe it did, but the Spartans still won the game. Tom had been frustrated about the seating situation in the Breslin Center and on that night he'd finally reached his boiling point.

In 1976, I worked the MSU at North Carolina State football

game on radio. The Spartans played to a 31-31 tie in a wild game featuring some big plays from Kirk Gibson. My color man went on the alumni tour earlier in the week and had played golf that morning. We met up in the afternoon at a pregame function where there was plenty of beer. He figured we might need it for the night so instead of filling his brief case with pregame notes, he filled it with crushed ice and about six beers. He didn't drink them all, but he had a couple and he actually sounded a bit more lively on the air than usual.

One day back in the 1980s, we asked well-known Lansing boxing coach Bob Every to predict the outcome of a big upcoming fight on the air. When I argued with him about his pick, he told us, "I'll jump off the Kalamazoo Street bridge if this guy loses." Natch his fighter lost.

Several days later, with cameras rolling and fans watching, Every jumped off the Kalamazoo Street Bridge into the cool Grand River. The police warned him never to do it again.

Another time, I was driving at night with Jim Hornberger to Indiana to televise an MSU vs. Indiana basketball game the next day. We were hungry so we stopped at a drive-through McDonald's shortly after we'd left. I ordered a McRib sandwich.

"Could I please have extra sauce on that?" I asked.

"You don't need extra sauce, do you Tim? Those things have enough on them to begin with," Jim warned.

Have you ever tried to eat a McRib sandwich and drive at the same time? Fifteen minutes down the road, in the darkness of the car, Jim said, "I smell barbecue sauce. Turn on the light."

To my horror, my shirt, tie and pants were covered with the stuff. I mean saturated. I smelled like a barbecue pit for the next three hours.

When we arrived in Bloomington, Detroit newspaper writer Lynn Henning bumped into us while we were checking in at the hotel.

"What in the world happened to you?" He was almost worried about me.

But the coup de gras occurred in September of 1997. I'd like to admit to making this up but it's all true.

After my 6 p.m. show one night, my wife asked me to pick up our son from football practice at 7:30 and bring him home. Figuring I had time to get the car washed, I headed for my regular service station. The top was down and I didn't want to go through all the hassle of a ratchet wrench to get it back on. The weather was good and after the wash I wanted to take the top back off while I drove over to the football field.

This was one of those deluxe drive-through washes. I placed the top on the car without securing it and figured if I didn't make it all the way through the wash I could always back out. No one was behind me. I was hoping the seals were water tight.

They were. The car went through the wash portion of its journey with no problems. Next up was the blow dryer. Now another car had pulled in behind me.

Disaster. When those blow dryers hit that car, the top got sucked up like a barn roof in the movie Twister. I mean it flew into the ceiling. I had papers laying over the passenger seat of the car and they all got blown away. I had water falling into the car, drenching the seats and me at the same time. I drove through it all, but now what was I to do about my top?

The woman behind me was calmly watching this entire show. I walked back through the dryers with my hair flying in the wind and my tie now pointing straight upward. I found some of my papers and I found the damaged top and walked out with them. I was mortified. I was also soaked.

The top was ruined (a $595 fee to my insurance company) , my car was soaked both outside and inside, and so was I. My tie was ruined. It seemed like such a good plan. The dorks of the world had just crowned a new king. None of it would have ever happened if only I'd taken a couple of minutes to ratchet down the top properly. Or if my wife had not called me to pick up our son, so I guess it's her fault, looking back.

And I can only wonder what that woman entering the car wash behind me must have thought witnessing it all. Had someone taped the scenario I'd have had one super blooper tape.

Local television stations today love to send reporters on location, be it near or far, to cover stories, live on the scene. Technology has made this an inexpensive option and news programs commonly use what are called "live shots." I think they tend to be over used—the same story could have been taped completely without a loss of quality. But stations see competitors use live shots and so it becomes a numbers game—who can do the most? Consultants tell stations the public loves live shots and so they are frequently seen.

I do not do many of these live shots for several reasons. They can be time consuming and they tend to prohibit other stories from making the air because of time constraints. I have always felt the more complicated any show becomes to produce, the greater chance there is for technical difficulties. The more people who have a hand in any program, the more opportunity there is for something to go wrong. Believe it.

One night several years ago, I was scheduled to call a basketball game in the Breslin Center at Michigan State. Since our production meeting would start at about 6:45, I decided to air my sportscast on location. Sure enough, the live truck was scheduled and it made its routine appearance about an hour before air time.

It usually takes about three technicians to assist on location—two in the truck and one cameraman. Sometimes they do not always travel to the location in the same vehicle.

On this night, the microphone was checked and the signal back to the station looked good. I was busy preparing for the game when I walked down to the end of the court before joining the news team on air with my segment. There were several cameras and personnel in the area and I never thought to check to make sure that my guy was in the group.

The time was about 5:55—air time for the sports would be about 6:23. Where was my camera man? The other camera operators noticed my distress and a quick cell phone call back to the office produced a gasp on the other end of the line—the assignment desk forgot to send a camera operator!

Now I am in big trouble. I have everything but a camera! One guy who would work the baseline camera for the game that night offered to patch his camera into our cable to see if that would work. That produced good news and bad news. The good news was we got a picture and sound. The bad news was there was no color—the units did not quite match. I had no choice. I would have to appear in black and white with wavy lines running through the picture. When these problems occur I mutter to myself about never going on location again.

Incredibly, one of our guys actually made it out the door of the studio in south Lansing and into the Breslin Center lot in 12 minutes. He raced into the arena some 60 seconds before air time and made the required hook up. His name was Tony Conley and he was an athletic guy, thank goodness. He had no tripod, so he had to hold the camera on his shoulder, all the while heaving back and forth trying to catch his breath.

Understand that it is tough enough to do location shots with no teleprompter and no privacy that you get in an enclosed studio. This was embarrassing to say the least. We looked like keystone cops getting on the air that night. The stress level rises as each minute goes by and airtime draws closer—with technical problems left to be solved.

Tony made a tremendous effort in difficult circumstances. In earlier years, I would have been a zombie afterward trying to find the guilty party. But once a broadcast is over there is little carry over effect to the next one. Realizing that, I don't go to pieces after problem broadcasts the way I did in my youth.

I took some razzing from my basketball telecast crew that night, but the bottom line was reached—the six o'clock sports still made the air the way it had been planned. Never mind the fact that it aged me a bit!

Even though sometimes I wonder, technical problems on live shots can occur anywhere at any time and even the networks can have their share of problems. Whenever I watch someone else struggling with a live shot I can only mutter, "Thank God that isn't me tonight!"

CHAPTER 17

Criticism

Familiarity breeds contempt. I don't know who said it, but I wonder if it applies to people. I sure hope not. I have been on the air in the same area for nearly 30 years now. I turn 50 in March 1999. My current boss was about eight years old when I first went on the air. It just worked out that I have used this market as my home base of operations. I have no idea how long I'll remain on the air and how long I will be on the air in mid-Michigan.

Elsewhere in this book I discuss the keys to staying on the air, or in anything else for that matter, for an extended period of time. I also discuss dealing with criticism. If you can't stand the heat, get out of the kitchen. Harry was right about that.

In my business there are two kinds of criticism—that which is deserved and that to which is not worth paying any attention. The difficulty is in determining which is which. I hear less criticism today than I did some years ago for several reasons.

When I began on television in 1971, there was no cable. In mid-Michigan, there was virtually only one credible news station—WJIM-TV Channel 6. Whatever you said on the air, many people tended to hear. Their alternatives for news were few. Sportscasters had more time to air their shows in those days, at least five minutes. Personal opinions, called commentaries, were the rage. In almost all markets, sportscasters would deliver their own editorials and most of them would be critical.

The upside to them was that you could get people to think, and you could add an edge to your show. If they were well-written and delivered, they tended to add some spice to the usual menu of highlights that tended to look the same night after night.

The downside was that they could infuriate people, both the public and whoever was your topic. Like today, Michigan State was the dominant news source in this area, so it was my number one topic. When I thought the school did something wrong, I told the public about it. In doing so, I caused a number of viewers to criticize my work.

The most criticism I ever received was after a commentary condemning Michigan State on the day it announced Muddy Waters would become the new head football coach in 1980. I said, "They blew it."

Simple as that. I felt his background would not transfer to the high pressure job he would be facing in the Big Ten. In hindsight, what I said turned out to be accurate. Muddy was fired after three years with a 10-23 career record. But at the time, my station received many letters, most of them well-written, criticizing my comments. If it was a tough time for Muddy, it was a tough time for me too. But I have only myself to blame. I was 31 years old at the time and while I had been on the air for ten years, I didn't consider what I said on the air then as I do today.

The local news business has changed. Sports time is usually four minutes or less so that means it's entertainment time. If what viewers see doesn't appeal to them, they can always hit that cable remote and find something more interesting. It's as easy as that. In my judgment, cable television is the cause of so much tabloid stuff being passed off as hard news today. Boring news just doesn't attract a large enough audience.

I very rarely do commentaries anymore and for a couple of reasons. First, people can get enough of my opinions each day on the radio. Secondly, I don't have as much time on the air anymore. Lastly, what I happen to think is not as valuable as what I show.

My criticism today comes mainly from those who think we should do more coverage of those things of interest to them. Most of it is from parents trying to sell us on a high school team for which their son or daughter just happens to play. I used to argue with these callers, but not anymore. I can give them legitimate reasons why they don't see what they want, but usually their minds are made up that I am wrong and they are right. It's not worth the bother.

Some critical calls are very good and can be very helpful.

Most complaint calls do not get through to me or I would never have time to finish a day's work. Some do and if I think the criticism has merit I thank the caller and take it to heart.

Some calls are so preposterous that you wonder who in the world belongs to the voice on the other end of the line.

"Mr. Staudt," the caller began on the phone one day last winter, "Why don't you cover Everett and Sexton basketball?"

"I don't know what you are referring to, but I can tell you that I can remember airing a number of highlights of those schools during this entire season," I immediately answered.

"It's probably because there are no white kids on those teams and you only cover schools with white players," she retorted, her voice now rising.

Just as I was telling her that I resented that charge, the phone slammed down on my ear. It was perhaps just as well. Who knows what astute retort I would have come up with next.

The problem with high school sports on television is that they appeal to a minor segment of the audience. Outside of the parents and students at high school X, who really cares to watch "highlights" of high school X's basketball team or any other team at that school, for that matter? Very few people, trust me.

That's not to say that the high schools do not provide good human interest stories—most all of them do. Finding them isn't always easy, but they're out there and they appeal to a vastly larger segment of the audience than just hard news game highlights.

I know of stations who flood the airwaves with countless high school highlights from all over the place. Then they promote their news by saying "we give you local coverage like no one else does." If quantity is the measuring stick, I will never measure up. Anyone can send photographers scurrying to numerous high school games, show two plays from each later that evening and call that "complete coverage."

How many people at home do you really think want to watch "highlights" of 15 high school football or basketball games, let alone any other sport? My guess is few. They want to watch their own son or daughter, or their own school, or maybe a highly-touted college recruit—but after that the audience interest is limited.

I don't get criticized at all over pro sports coverage anymore. In outstate markets, it seems that the interest level in major league sports is considerably less than it once was. The money pro athletes make, I believe, has turned off many people outside the large urban areas. I almost never get a complaint about too few Tiger highlights or too few Pistons highlights. Not as I did in earlier years anyway.

If you criticize the universities on the air, you find some thin skin. But if you are fair, it isn't that big a deal. One problem is sportscasters covering athletes who get into trouble with the law. In the 1970s these stories were covered as sports news.

Today I have managed to hand off most of these athletes-in-trouble-with-the-law stories to the news department. I don't need to use up my precious air time on these when the news people can cover them. I don't need the constant strained relations these stories cause between athletes, their coaches, and myself. I'm also not sure if they all merit extensive coverage in the first place.

News departments tend to have trouble catching their breath when a football player gets arrested for drunk driving. How much some of these college athletes come under the category of "public figures" is open to debate. A single story is one thing—some of them run day after day after day. Is the public all that interested in non-stop coverage? You tell me.

I have finally accepted the fact that no one on the air can please 100 percent of the audience at any one time. It is simply impossible to do. The American public has too many diverse opinions for one person to appease them all.

Those of us on the air don't like criticism any more than coaches do, but it goes with the territory. Experience is the best remedy for dealing with it. The older you get, the better you learn how to accept criticism for what it is worth—to discard that which is frivolous and to use constructively that which has merit.

In any live, ad lib situation, one wrong word can cause a torrent of criticism. In the early 1980s, I was reporting one spring night on how tough Michigan State's baseball team was having it. I mentioned that the Spartans had lost that day to "lowly" Albion. The meaning was that Albion's team wasn't very good either and that a major Division I school like Michigan State couldn't even beat a Division III club that does not give scholarships. But the word "lowly" was seen as denigrating to the entire Albion College family.

I got blasted in a couple of newspapers—one even said I should be fired over that comment. I heard plenty from the Albion people. My intent was not mean-spirited, but it came out sounding very demeaning to a number of people. In hindsight, it was one of the worst words I could ever have come up with for that story. It is an incident I often remember, and not fondly either.

Last winter, I aired a two-hour live March Madness hockey and basketball special. During one portion of the program we were showing live shots of a high school basketball game. The score was very uneven and the game was nearing an end.

"Let's dump out of this game," I said. "The scrubs are in now and the outcome has been decided."

I never thought twice at the time about using the word "scrubs." But we got complaint calls all night. I went on the air during the 11 o'clock news and said something like I never was very smart and if I offended anyone during our earlier show this evening with the word 'scrubs,' then I apologize. In hindsight, it wasn't that big of a gaffe, but the older I get the more I realize some people get offended by remarks that I don't think are improper—but if you are trying to enlarge your audience and not decrease it—it is wise to always try and cover your bases.

I have no idea if my apology was accepted or not by those who called, but it was the best I could do. I've become more conscious of what I do and say in public over the years. Perception is reality, right? It is easier for me to change myself than to try and change others.

Criticism can be a very good character builder. You face yourself in the mirror each day and you either tell yourself you are doing the best you can, or you feel self-pity or even like you are a scapegoat. How you look at yourself and how you handle criticism can either help or hurt the things you want to accomplish in life.

I've decided to take what criticism comes and, as George Perles always used to say, "take a negative and try to turn it into a positive."

CHAPTER 18

Longevity

I have always been impressed with people who have longevity. Either they lived a long life, or they enjoyed a long career. It is difficult, especially in today's ever changing world, to achieve longevity.

I have been blessed with longevity to the degree that I have been on the air in Mid-Michigan for nearly 30 years. When people ask me what I am most proud of about my career, I always tell them without hesitation that it is being on the air longer than any other personality in Mid-Michigan broadcasting. Talent is a subjective issue—the public has widely differing opinions on who is talented and who is not.

When Michigan State hosted Miami of Florida in football a few years ago, I attended the Hurricanes' Friday pre-game practice. Several Miami reporters knew who I was and they were telling me if they had to do their careers over, they would have stayed in "one market like you have." These guys had made several career stops to get to a big city like Miami. I told them I never planned on where I would end up; it all had just worked out by chance. I have had opportunities to work in other markets, and for different reasons have turned them down and stayed put. I never say never to any opportunity, but I have never wished my days away hoping I'd find something bigger and better.

In 1978 I was offered the sports directorship at WHIO-TV in Dayton, Ohio. It was a very good station, where talk show host Phil Donahue got his start. I would have accepted the offer but for one reason—the news director wanted me to work Saturday nights in addition to anchoring all of the weeknight sportscasts. In those days, stations did not have large sports staffs as they do today. I thought about it and thought about it and finally decided this would be a lateral move—so I turned it down.

In 1982, I attracted the attention of Chicago agent Todd Musburger. He is the brother of ABC sportscaster Brent Musburger. Todd serves as Brent's agent today. Todd landed a great job offer for me—weekends at WMAQ-TV in Chicago, the NBC-owned and operated station. It was a tremendous prospect and included a radio deal. At the time I was going through some personal turmoil and wasn't completely thinking the way I might today. After agonizing over this for a couple of days, I finally turned it down simply because the timing was not right. Offers like that don't come along often and I brooded over my decision for days afterward. Ironically, the station promoted the guy it eventually hired to the number one job a month later when that position opened. The money would have been incredible. And who knows where I would be today.

A year later I met my wife. Had I have taken that job I likely would never have met her and, therefore, would not have the three boys I have today. I certainly do not regret turning down that offer today. Did the good Lord have a plan for me that I was not aware of at the time?

I have always admired people with longevity: Walter Cronkite's run at CBS; Bobby Knight's tenure at Indiana and Dean Smith's at North Carolina; Bob Hope entertaining America—you get the point.

I believe there are key components to achieving longevity in anything. I now offer you my ten commandments of longevity— I tell students my theories when I speak to them and I have carefully considered these suggestions over the years.

1) You must be good with people. You must have respect for everyone you come in contact with in your organization. You want people to like and respect you. You never want anyone to think that you are above them. To achieve longevity, you need allies, not enemies.

2) You need a sense of humor. After love, I consider humor the greatest gift God gives us. Some people are funnier than others, but everyone can have a sense of humor. Life is too short to be constantly confrontational. People enjoy being around people who find humor in the world.

3) Take others seriously but not yourself. This is a Duffy Daugherty commandment and he lived it to the fullest. Duffy had many, many friends. He had a great sense of humor and he was very good at poking fun at himself. When you take yourself too seriously, life is full of tension. Who needs it?

4) Be willing to compromise. You must pick your battles and there should not be very many. When in doubt, compromise. You don't have to let people walk all over you, but you should show a willingness to meet others halfway when there is a legitimate dispute.

5) Control your ego. Egos are important. Without one you have little self confidence and respect for yourself. You want to strive to do well and if you do, you should be proud of it—but no one likes to be around an egomaniac. Remember you want allies, not enemies.

6) Be well organized. There are only so many hours in your day and only so many of those hours find you at your peak. There is no time to waste because you are unorganized. You do not want to make mistakes because of your own carelessness.

7) Be forgiving. You must depend on others in your life for many different reasons and no one is perfect. If someone makes a mistake that costs you, remember you may need them to help you again. If you forgive, they likely will not forget. They'll owe you one, so to speak. You look bigger in someone's eyes who has made a mistake when you forgive.

8) Show your appreciation. Never take people for granted. Thank them when it is deserved. Go out of your way in these areas. People will gravitate to you more willingly with this kind of attitude.

9) Be honest. If you are deceitful once, you likely will be again. Honesty should be the hallmark of everything you do. You want people to know they can always trust you.

10) You need the good Lord in your life. By Sunday, I'm spiritually worn out from the week. I need to be reminded that I can handle all of the problems in life I face. You can't do that depending on yourself or other human beings alone. Find a religion in which you find peace and comfort. Don't do it to pay your dues—do it because you have faith and it means something to you. Don't be ashamed to tell others how you feel. If you have a legitimate religious faith, absolutely nothing will ever get the best of

you in the long run.

I am not about to tell you that my ten commandments are the sole reasons I have lasted 30 years in broadcasting. But they sure haven't hurt either.

EPILOGUE

In June of 1997, I took my oldest son, Tom, with me to the Sunday afternoon portion of the Children's Miracle Network telethon at Lansing's Sparrow Hospital. Over the years, my assignment at this event has mainly been to help anchor the call-in portion in front of a tote board. While that segment of the telecast is crucial in raising funds, it is not my favorite role. Several years ago, I asked to be assigned to the children's ward. I wanted to go to the scene of the problems and meet some of these unfortunate children and their parents. I felt more valuable in sharing their stories and their plight directly to the public rather than just pleading for people to pick up their phones and call in a pledge.

On this particular day, I made my first visit to Sparrow's burn ward. Tom and I were ordered to wash up and wear gowns and masks. We were taken to a room by Dr. Stephen Guertin to meet Danny Tice, a youngster from Jackson.

The day before, Danny, at only 8 years old, nearly died in a camper fire near Cadillac. His entire family was burned in an explosion of a propane gas stove. His father went back into the camper and pulled his son to safety, saving his life.

The other members of the family did not suffer severe injuries, but Danny was in serious to critical condition. When I met him he was covered with bandages, crying and in great pain. I could hardly keep my composure trying to visit with him. He was clearly scared. He was also depressed because he lost his baseball bat and glove in the accident.

I decided to take my son with me to show him what a great gift he has been given in having good health. I intend to take my other two boys as they get a bit older. My kids not only are healthy, they have a nice home and loving parents—they are truly blessed.

The plan called for me to interview Danny Tice from the hospital, for five minutes, during the telethon. I would also get comments from his parents and Dr. Guertin. It was one of the toughest assignments I have ever been called on to handle. It took every ounce of resolve I could muster to get through the interviews because I had trouble composing myself. Listening to that poor child's cries of pain would get to anyone.

I tell this story because my advice to you is that when you think your life is a downer, you can still find much for which to be thankful. My motto in life has always been: "Count your blessings, not your desires." We can all wish for our lives to be more enriched to various degrees, but I find the happiest people are those who count their blessings.

I have been blessed in so many ways I don't know where to begin to offer thanks. There have been very few days in my life in which I have faced crisis. As one gets older, I suspect the more appreciation one feels when he or she is richly blessed.

I was fortunate to land a job I love right out of college. I was always a number one anchor—I never had to "pay my dues" working under someone else in the lead sportscaster position. I have enjoyed many great experiences and met many great people along the way. I don't know where it will all end, but it has been a heckuva ride.

In my youth, sports used to practically be the reason for my existence. Looking back, there are issues which I believe I took way too seriously on the air. In hindsight, I wish I would have smiled more and not made quite so many judgments. I don't know what my future holds. I do know that I appreciate this community and my chance to be a part of it. I hope I can contribute to it for many more years to come.

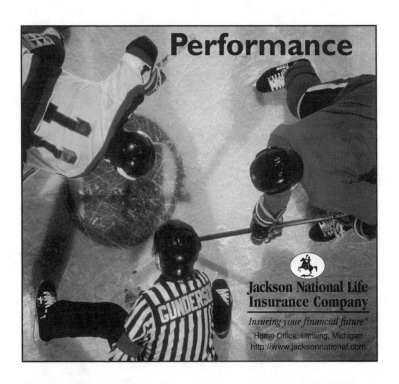

Performance

Jackson National Life Insurance Company

Insuring your financial future.

Home Office: Lansing, Michigan
http://www.jacksonnational.com

Staudt on Sports

VISIONS

Cover design by: Camron Gnass

Edited by: Lisa Gagarin

Printed in USA

ISBN 0-9658933-9-1

51995

EAN

9 780965 893398

$19.95